Herbert Puchta, Jeff Stranks and Peter Lewis-Jones

English in Mind

* Student's Book 4

CAMBRIDGE
UNIVERSITY PRESS

Speaking & functions	Listening	Reading	Writing
Talking about special talents	Interview with a psychologist about autistic savants	Blind Tom and Stephen Wiltshire Literature: *The Curious Incident of the Dog in the Night-time*	Narrative (1)
Talking about people's problems and feelings	Discussion about flower remedies	Placebos Prove Powerful Remedies from the Rainforest Story: Eyes open	Article for a school magazine
Talking about the way our brains work Discussing sport Discussing the nature of intelligence	Interview with two sportswomen	They Just Can't Help It Culture: Intelligence Across Cultures	Discursive essay (1)
Talking about time	Interview about Doctor Who Song: *If I Could Turn Back Time*	Quiz about Doctor Who Letter giving advice	Informal letter
Discussing shyness Talking about personal qualities	Interview with an expert on shyness	Questionnaire: How confident are you? Literature: *Pride and Prejudice*	Description of a person
Organising a flash mob	Interview with someone who organises flash mobs	Text about crazes from the past Story: Sorry!	Letter to a newspaper
Talking about acts of kindness Asking questions using modals Talking about birthdays	People talking about special objects they have inherited	Hit-and-Run Kindness Culture: Birthday Traditions	A summary
Resolving conflicts	Interview about Wangari Maathai Song: *Peace, Love and Understanding*	Alfred Nobel Rests in Peace	Appreciation of a Nobel Prize winner
Discussing age limits in the UK / your country	A radio phone-in programme about giving the vote to 16-year-olds	Weblog about a trip to Mount Everest Literature: *Lord of the Flies*	Letter raising money for charity
Discussing global issues Discussing ways of conserving energy	Radio programme about alternative energy	Time's Running Out Story: The factory	Write a magazine article about the future
Expressing opinions Discussing the role of music concerts in raising awareness of global issues	People's views on famous people getting involved in politics	Celebrity Ambassadors Culture: Can Music Make a Difference?	Discursive essay (2)
Discussing Fair Trade products	The Village Earth Song: *I'd Like to Teach the World to Sing*	Young People Leading the Way on Fair Trade	Report on a class survey
Discussing language and accents	TV programme about regional accents	Near-Extinct Language Returns Literature: *The World According to Garp*	Narrative (2)
Describing an interesting trip	Account of a trip to the Grand Canyon	Three texts about wonderful places in the world Story: Round the world	Description of a place
Discussing films and 'film therapy'	Conversation about films	Movie Therapy Culture: Planet Bollywood	Film synopsis
Discussing the effect music has on you Discussing which music you like/dislike	Radio programme about musical instruments from round the world Song: *Lost in Music*	A World of Music	Haikus/limericks/ mini-sagas

YOU WILL LEARN ABOUT ...

- 'Autistic savants' – people of unique talent ....
- The powerful healing effects of the human mind ....
- Plants from the Amazon used for medical purposes ....
- Differences in male and female brains ....
- Women in 'male' sports ....
- A cult BBC TV programme called Doctor Who ....

* Can you match each picture with a topic?

YOU WILL LEARN HOW TO ...

Speak
- Talk about special talents
- Discuss mind matters
- Talk about medicines
- Talk about psychological problems
- Discuss a theory about different brain types
- Talk about sports
- Talk about a piece of advice or a recommendation

Write
- A story that begins or ends with a given sentence
- An article for a school magazine
- A composition about a sport
- An informal letter

Read
- An article about people with outstanding brain capacities
- Placebos prove powerful
- An article about the secret knowledge of tribal medicine men
- A newspaper article about the human brain
- A worried teenager's letter to her dad

Listen
- A radio interview with a psychologist
- A conversation about flower remedies
- Interviews with sports professionals about their jobs
- A radio show on a cult TV programme

Use grammar

Can you match the names of the grammar points with the examples?

Past tense	Biological mechanisms **have been discovered** through new techniques.
Present Perfect tense	I love reading, **which is why I buy so many books**.
Passive	He **said that** his health was getting worse.
Passive continuous	He **began** to realise that Stephen **was communicating** through drawings.
Relative clauses	A new generation of painkillers **is being developed**.
Reported speech	Since then he **has published** a number of books.

Use vocabulary

Can you think of two more examples for each topic?

Expressions with *mind*	Operations and illness	Sports	Expressions with *time*
make up (your) mind	doctor	tennis	waste time
change (your) mind	give an injection	racket	run out of time
....	....	....	....
....	....	....	....

1 Super brains

* Tense revision
* Vocabulary: expressions with *mind*
* Vocabulary: expressions with *brain*

1 Read and listen

(a) What do you think the two boys in the pictures have in common? Read the texts to check your ideas.

In 1850 an American lawyer, James N. Bethune, bought a slave to work in his home. The slave, a woman, had a small child called Tom, who was blind and autistic.

One day, Bethune was walking around his garden when he heard music coming from the house. He went inside to investigate and found young Tom playing on the family piano. Bethune realised that the boy, who was only four, had special abilities. He hired a band of musicians to come to the house and play in front of him. Tom reproduced perfectly the music he had heard. This confirmed Bethune's suspicion – Tom had the ability to memorise and repeat pieces of music after hearing them just once.

In 1857 'Blind Tom', as he was called from then on, took part in his first public performance. The reviews were so good that Bethune took him on a tour of the US. Three years later, Blind Tom was invited to the White House, where he performed for the president. Over the next forty years, Tom performed shows all over the US, as well as visiting Canada, the UK and several South American countries. His concerts were a mixture of classical music and his own compositions. They also featured a section called the 'challenge' when members of the audience played a piece of music on the piano which Tom then had to reproduce. He never failed. Blind Tom died in 1908.

Stephen Wiltshire was born in 1974 in London. He was mute (unable to speak) and, at the age of three, was diagnosed with autism, a developmental disorder causing difficulty with social relationships and learning. However, Stephen has a remarkable talent. Since the age of three, he has been creating the most amazing drawings. He is an 'autistic savant' – a person who, in spite of his autism, has an extraordinary ability in a certain area.

When his mother sent him to Queensmill School in London, his teacher, Chris Marris, began to realise that Stephen was 'communicating' through his drawings. At the age of eight, he was drawing detailed pictures of architecture, cars and imaginary post-earthquake cities. By the age of nine, with Marris' help, Stephen started talking. At the age of ten, he produced a series of pictures which he called 'London Alphabet'. Each drawing featured a London landmark – one for each letter of the alphabet.

After Stephen and his work were the subject of a BBC programme called 'The Foolish Wise Ones' in 1987, many viewers phoned the BBC. They were fascinated by Stephen's ability to look at a building once and reproduce it in incredible detail, and wanted to know where they could buy his drawings. As a result, Stephen published his first book, *Drawings*. Since then, Stephen has become an extremely popular artist, and has published a number of other books of his drawings and paintings.

Stephen is quite famous these days. Because of Stephen and others like him, people are starting to take autism more seriously.

(b) 🔊 Read the texts again and listen. Complete the table.

	Blind Tom	Stephen Wiltshire
1 What is/was his special ability?	....	....
2 Who helped him develop this ability?	....	....
3 How did he become famous?	....	....
4 What examples are given of his success?	....	....

2 Speak

Work in groups. Look at the list below and discuss the following:

● Do you have a special talent for any of these things? At what age did you realise you were good at it/them?

● Can you name a well-known person who has (or had) a special talent in each area?

● Which two areas would you most like to have a special talent for? Say why.

language	music
memory	sport
mathematics	dance/movement
art	cooking

3 Grammar

Present tense review

a Look at the text about Stephen Wiltshire again. Underline:

one example of the *present simple* tense.
one example of the *present continuous* tense.
two examples of the *present perfect* tense.
one example of the *present perfect continuous* tense.

Why do you think each tense is used?

b Complete the sentences about Stephen Wiltshire with the verbs in brackets. Use the correct form of the tenses in Exercise 3a.

1 Stephen ____lives____ (live) in West London with his mother.

2 Some of the books that Stephen _____ (write) include *Cities, Floating Cities* and *Stephen Wiltshire's American Dream.*

3 I'm not sure what Stephen Wiltshire is doing at the moment, but he _____ probably _____ (draw) something.

4 Since 1993, Stephen _____ (develop) his musical skills, which are also quite amazing.

5 Since Stephen first met the famous neurologist, Oliver Sachs, in 1988, the two men _____ (become) good friends.

6 Stephen _____ (have) a sister, Annette, who is two years older than him.

Past tense review

c Look back at the text about Blind Tom and underline:

two examples of the *past simple* tense.
one example of the *past continuous* tense.
one example of the *past perfect* tense.

Why do you think each tense is used?

d Circle the correct option to complete the sentences.

1 As well as the piano, Tom also *learned / was learning* to play the flute and the French horn.

2 One day Tom *was playing / played* the piano when a man ran onto the stage and tried to stop him.

3 Two songs that Blind Tom *wrote / had written* are *The Rainstorm* and *Battle of Manassas.*

4 Tom always *was saying / said* that his songs came from the river, the trees and the birds.

5 By the time he died in 1908, Tom *learned / had learned* to play more than 7,000 pieces of music.

e Complete the text using the correct form of the verbs in brackets. Use the tenses in Exercises 3a and 3c.

When Brittany Maier was born she was blind and autistic. By the time she was five, she still [1]_____ (not learn) to speak, but she suddenly [2]_____ (begin) to sing while she [3]_____ (listen) to a song on her parents' stereo. Brittany is now a young adult. Over the years, she [4]_____ (learn) to talk a little, but she still [5]_____ (find) it difficult to communicate through language. Her music teacher, a professor at the university of South Carolina, [6]_____ (work) with Brittany for five years now. He says that she is unique. She [7]_____ (play) with only six fingers, but she has the musical qualities of Beethoven, Mozart and Chopin.

4 Vocabulary

Expressions with *mind*

(a) 🔊 Match the definitions 1–10 with the expressions a–j. Use a dictionary if you need to. Then listen, check and repeat.

1 make a new and different decision
2 help you not to think about a problem
3 try not to forget about something
4 decide
5 forget
6 be crazy
7 find it hard to decide
8 say what you think
9 try to know what another person is thinking
10 be worried

a make up (your) mind
b change (your) mind
c be in two minds
d be out of (your) mind
e have got (something) on (your) mind
f keep (something) in mind
g speak (your) mind
h read (someone's) mind
i take (your) mind off (something)
j slip (your) mind

(b) Complete the sentences with the expressions from Exercise 4a. (Make sure you use the correct verb form.)

1 A: 'You look worried.'
   B: 'Yes, I am a little. I've __got something on my mind__ at the moment.'

2 A: 'I'm not sure ... should I buy the red one or the blue one?'
   B: 'I don't care! But please, _____ !'

3 A: 'But you said you'd come with me!'
   B: 'I know. I'm sorry, but now I don't want to come. I've _____.'

4 A: 'So ... do you still want to go out tonight?'
   B: 'Well, maybe. I _____ about it.'

5 A: 'But you promised to do it.'
   B: 'I'm sorry, I forgot. It just _____.'

6 A: 'Aren't you worried about the exam?'
   B: 'Yes, a little bit. So I'm going to relax and watch a good film. That will _____ off it.'

7 A: 'Well, that's what I think you should do.'
   B: 'OK, thanks, it's good advice. I'll _____.'

8 A: 'I'm really angry with him, but I don't want to tell him.'
   B: 'I think you should. Sometimes it's important to _____.'

9 'If you don't tell me, I won't know. I can't _____.'

10 A: 'I'm going rock climbing tomorrow.'
   B: 'What? Are you _____ ? It's really dangerous!'

5 Speak

Work with a partner. Ask and answer questions.

1 In which situations do you find it difficult to make up your mind?
2 In which situations do you usually find it easy/difficult to speak your mind?
3 If you are worried about something, what do you do to take your mind off the problem?
4 Are you good at reading other people's minds? If so, what helps you?

6 Listen

(a) Work with a partner. Complete the number sequences.

A 2, 3, 5, 7, 11, 13, 17, 19, 23, ..., ..., ...

B 2–4, 3–9, 4–16, 7–49, ...–100, ...–144, ...–625

(b) Are they *square roots* or *prime numbers*?

(c) You are going to listen to an interview with a psychologist about *autistic savants*. What things do you think *autistic savants* might be good at remembering?

(d) 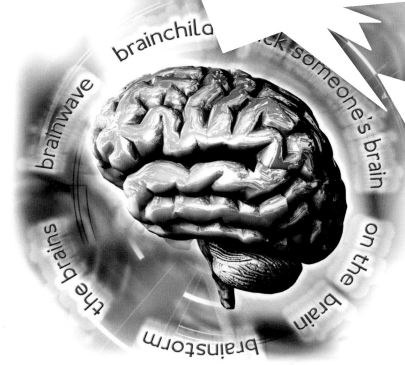 Listen and check your ideas.

(e) ◁)) Listen again and answer the questions.

1 What are the most common forms of autistic abilities?

2 What does the psychologist say about square roots and prime numbers?

3 What is the ratio of boys to girls who are diagnosed to be *autistic savants*?

4 What is the percentage of autistic people who are also *savants*?

5 'The brains of *autistic savants* are just like ours.' What is the significance of this, according to Dr Sellers?

7 Vocabulary

Expressions with *brain*

(a) Read the dialogues. Match the <u>underlined</u> expressions with definitions 1–6.

1 think of as many ideas as you can
   brainstorm

2 get ideas from someone ....

3 brilliant idea ....

4 original idea or invention ....

5 the (most) intelligent person
   ....

6 to always think about the same thing
   ....

1 A: Mum, I'm stuck with my English homework.
   B: Why don't you <u>pick your sister's brains</u>? She's good at English.

2 A: What's up, Jane? You're day-dreaming again.
   B: I'm thinking about Simon ....
   A: <u>You've got boys on the brain</u>. Yesterday, it was Chris!

3 A: I can't think of anything to write.
   B: Let's <u>brainstorm</u> some ideas together then.

4 A: You did well in the maths test, Ali.
   B: Not as well as Gill, she got 90%. She's <u>the brains</u> in our class!

5 A: I'm bored. What are we going to do? It's still pouring with rain.
   B: I've had a <u>brainwave</u>! Why don't we give Steve a ring and see if he wants to go to the cinema?

6 A: The recycling project is doing fantastically well.
   B: Yes, it is, thanks to Michelle. It was her <u>brainchild</u>.

(b) Use the expressions in Exercise 7a to complete these sentences.

1 Music! That's all you ever think about. You've .... music ....

2 If you don't know the answer, don't ask my father! Ask my mother. She's .... in the family.

3 I've just had a .... – and I think I've got the answer to my problem!

4 I built the machine. But it was Steve who had the idea and designed it. So it's his ....

5 Joe – I need help with this. Can I .... your .... for a moment?

6 We really need to get some new ideas. Let's all sit down and .... for a while.

8 Pronunciation

/ð/ *the* and /θ/ *thing*

◁)) Turn to page 120.

Literature in mind

9 Read

(a) Look at the cover of the book and read the short summary of the story. Would you be interested in reading this book? Why / why not?

THE CURIOUS INCIDENT of THE DOG IN THE NIGHT-TIME
By Mark Haddon

This is a murder mystery novel like no other. The detective, and narrator, is Christopher Boone. Christopher has Asperger's Syndrome. He knows a great deal about maths and very little about human beings. He loves lists, patterns and the truth. He hates the colours yellow and brown and being touched. He has never gone further than the end of the road on his own, but when he finds a neighbour's dog murdered he sets out on a terrifying journey which will turn his whole world upside down.

Then the police arrived. I like the police. They have uniforms and numbers and you know what they are meant to be doing. There was a policewoman and a policeman. The policewoman had a little hole in her tights and a red scratch in the middle of the hole. The policeman had a big orange leaf stuck to the bottom of his shoe which was poking out from one side.

The policewoman put her arms round Mrs. Shears and led her back toward the house.

I lifted my head off the grass.

The policeman squatted down beside me and said, "Would you like to tell me what's going on here, young man?"

I sat up and said, "The dog is dead."

"I'd got that far," he said.

I said, "I think someone killed the dog."

"How old are you?" he asked.

I replied, "I am 15 years and 3 months and 2 days."

"And what, precisely, were you doing in the garden?" he asked.

"I was holding the dog," I replied.

"And why were you holding the dog?" he asked.

This was a difficult question. It was something I wanted to do. I like dogs. It made me sad to see that the dog was dead.

I like policemen, too, and I wanted to answer the question properly, but the policeman did not give me enough time to work out the correct answer.

"Why were you holding the dog?" he asked again.

"I like dogs," I said.

"Did you kill the dog?" he asked.

"I did not kill the dog."

"Is this your fork?" he asked.

I said, "No."

"You seem very upset about this," he said.

He was asking too many questions and he was asking them too quickly. They were stacking up in my head like loaves in the factory where Uncle Terry works. The factory is a bakery and he operates the slicing machines. And sometimes a slicer is not working fast enough but the bread keeps coming and there is a blockage. I sometimes think of my mind as a machine, but not always as a bread-slicing machine. It makes it easier to explain to other people what is going on inside it.

The policeman said, "I am going to ask you once again ..."

I rolled back onto the lawn and pressed my forehead to the ground again and made the noise that Father calls groaning. I make this noise when there is too much information coming into my head from the outside world. It is like when you are upset and you hold the radio against your ear and you tune it halfway between two stations so that all you get is white noise and then you turn the volume right up so that this is all you can hear and then you know you are safe because you cannot hear anything else.

The policeman took hold of my arm and lifted me onto my feet.

I didn't like him touching me like this.

And this is when I hit him.

(b) Read the text quickly. What have the police come to investigate?

(c) Read the text again and answer the questions.

1 Why does Christopher like the police?

2 What is special about his ability to notice things about other people?

3 How old is Christopher? What is unusual about the way he talks about age?

4 How did Christopher feel when the policeman was asking him questions?

5 How does Christopher react when he is given too much information?

6 How does the author let us see inside Christopher's mind?

Discussion box

Work in pairs or small groups. Discuss these questions together.

1 Christopher hit the policeman. What might have been the reason(s) for his behaviour?

2 Should Christopher be punished for hitting the policeman? Why (not)?

10 Write

(a) In a writing competition, participants had to write a story beginning with the sentence below. Read the winning entry and answer the questions.

The worry of losing the money had been at the back of her mind all day.

1 How did Veronica feel at the beginning of the story?

2 How did she feel at the end of the story?

(b) Find time expressions in the story telling the reader when things happened.

All morning,... At first,...

(c) Write a story beginning with the sentence below. Use the model story to help you.

A minute after Christina had entered the room, she knew something was wrong.

Before you start writing your story, think about these questions. Use time expressions. Write 120–180 words.

- Who is Christina? How old is she?
- What is her background?
- How did she know something was wrong?
- What did she see, hear or feel?
- What actions did she take?
- How did the story end?

The worry of losing the money had been at the back of her mind all day. That was why she had not allowed herself for a single moment to let go of the yellow plastic bag that had the envelope in it, the one that her boss had given her. All morning, she had held it tight, and when she suddenly noticed that the bag was gone she was in a state of shock.

At first, Veronica didn't know what to do. She thought about all the people she had seen on the train that morning. There was one face she could not get out of her mind – the face of a tall young man. Suddenly, she was sure. "It was him, that tall young man who bumped into me after I got off the train! I'm going to find you!," Veronica thought, "if it's the last thing I do today!"

Veronica remembered the direction she had seen the young man take. She ran to the end of the platform and up the stairs towards Oxford Street. Two hours later, she was still in Oxford Street, and there was no sign of the young man, nor of the yellow bag. Veronica was looking at herself in a shop window. "Why was I so stupid?" she thought. And suddenly, she saw a reflection of the tall young man. There he was, on the opposite side of the street! He was talking to a young woman, and he was holding a yellow plastic bag in his hand! Without a moment's thought, Veronica dashed over to the two young people. "Give me my money back!" she yelled. By now, she had grabbed the plastic bag and both the young man and Veronica were wrestling with it. Neither of them wanted to let go of it.

A few seconds later, a police officer appeared. Veronica told him what had happened. "I'm afraid you've got it all wrong!" the officer said. "You must have dropped the bag when you were getting off the train. Your money is waiting for you at the police station – thanks to a very honest young person!" Veronica was speechless. She knew immediately what had happened. The man had found the plastic bag, and had taken the envelope with the money to the police! "Why did you keep the plastic bag?" she wanted to shout. But she didn't. The situation was too embarrassing for her!

2 Mind over matter

* Passive review
* Continuous passive forms
* Vocabulary: health and medical treatment
* Vocabulary: feelings

1 Read and listen

(a) What is a placebo? Read the text quickly to find out.

Placebos Prove Powerful

By SANDRA BLAKESLEE

Many doctors know the story of 'Mr Wright'. In 1957 he was diagnosed with cancer, and given only days to live. He had tumours the size of oranges. He heard that scientists had discovered a new medication, Krebiozen, that was effective against cancer, and he begged the doctor to give it to him. His physician, Dr Philip West, finally agreed. After Mr Wright had been given an injection on a Friday afternoon, the astonished doctor found his patient out of his 'death bed', joking with the nurses the following Monday. 'The tumours,' the doctor wrote later, 'had melted like snow balls on a hot stove.'

Two months later, Wright read medical reports that the medication was fake. His condition immediately got worse again. 'Don't believe what you read in the papers,' the doctor told Wright. Then he injected him with what he said was 'a new super-refined double strength' version of the drug. Actually, there was no drug, just a mix of salt and water, but again the tumours melted. Wright was the picture of health for another two months until he read an official report saying that Krebiozen was worthless. He died two days later.

This story has been ignored by doctors for a long time, dismissed as one of those strange tales that medicine cannot explain. The idea that a patient's beliefs can make a fatal disease go away has been thought of as too strange. But now scientists are discovering that the placebo effect is more powerful than anyone had ever thought. They are also beginning to discover how such miraculous results are achieved. Through new techniques of brain imagery, it can

be shown that a thought, a belief or a desire can cause chemical processes in the brain which can have powerful effects on the body. Scientists are learning that some body reactions are not caused by information coming into the brain from the outside world, but by what the brain expects to happen next.

Placebos are 'lies that heal,' said Dr Anne Harrington, a historian of science at Harvard University. 'The word placebo is Latin for "I shall please" (or I shall make you happy) and it is typically a treatment that a doctor gives to anxious patients to please them,' she said. 'It looks like medication, but has no healing ingredients whatsoever.' Nowadays, doctors have much more effective medicines to fight disease. But these treatments have not diminished the power of the placebo, quite the opposite. Maybe when scientists fully understand how placebos work, the powerful healing effects of the human mind will be used more systematically!

(b) 🔊 Read the text again and listen. Answer the questions.

1 What effect did the first injection have on Mr Wright?
2 What caused Mr Wright's death, according to the story?
3 What have been doctors' reactions to the story and why?
4 What new findings are there these days about the placebo effect?

Discussion box

Work in pairs or small groups. Discuss these questions together.

1 Do you believe that *placebos* can have a healing effect?
2 Do you think people or animals should be used to test medicines? Why / why not?

2 Grammar

Passive forms review

a Look at the text again. Underline the following in different colours. Then complete the rule. Use *by, to be, perfect, will, won't* and *past participle*.

Two examples of the *present simple* passive.
Two examples of the *present perfect* passive.
Two examples of the *past simple* passive.
One example of the *past perfect* passive.
One example of the *future* passive.

Rule:
- We form the present and past simple passive with a form of the verb .... and the ....
- The present perfect passive is formed with the present .... form of the verb ....
- The past perfect passive is formed with the past .... form of the verb ....
- The future passive is formed with .... or .... *be*, and the ....
- We use the preposition .... to say who or what does the action, but only if this is important.

b Complete the sentences with the correct passive form of the verb in brackets.

1 I've not been feeling well for some time, so I *'ve been given* (give) some mild medication.
2 When James was 12, he .... (diagnose) with appendicitis.
3 Penicillin .... (discover) by Alexander Fleming in 1928 and .... (test) for the first time on mice in 1940.
4 Over the next few years, lots of research .... (do) to find new medications.
5 Placebo effects .... (cause) by the power of the human mind, and not by medication.
6 The doctors discovered that the patient .... (give) the wrong medication for more than a year.

3 Vocabulary

Health and medicine

a 🔊 Match definitions 1–10 with expressions a–j. Listen and check.

1 to cut someone's body open to repair, remove or replace a damaged part
2 a drug that stops you from feeling pain in a part of the body
3 to become well again
4 a drug that makes you sleep during an operation so you do not feel pain
5 a special room in which people are operated on in a hospital
6 a doctor's judgement about what problem or illness a patient has
7 experience physical or mental pain
8 a doctor who has special training to carry out operations
9 a sign of illness in the body
10 a medical examination to test your state of health

a surgeon
b operating theatre
c to operate on (s.o.)
d a check-up
e symptom
f diagnosis
g general anaesthetic
h local anaesthetic
i to suffer (from)
j to recover (from)

b Read the sentences and complete them with the correct form of the words from Exercise 3a.

1 If she is worried about her health, she should see a doctor and get a thorough ....
2 My father was .... a week ago, but he's already in great shape again.
3 Claire's father will be operated on by a .... who specialises in knee joints.
4 A: Will he have to get .... when they operate on his toe?
  B: No, I don't think so. The doctor said .... will do!
5 She had very bad flu. It took her almost three weeks to .... it.
6 The doctor hasn't given her the .... yet, but she doesn't think she's seriously ill.
7 The operation was very complicated. The patient was in the .... for six hours!
8 She's got all the .... of a bad cold: a high temperature, a headache and a sore throat.
9 Sandra .... from terrible headaches at the moment.

4 Pronunciation

Consonant clusters

🔊 Turn to page 120.

5 Read

(a) Discuss the questions. Read the text and check your ideas.

1. How do you think indigenous tribes of the Amazon rainforest treated illnesses over the centuries?
2. Why do you think the knowledge of Indian healers is important to scientists today?

(b) Read the text again. Answer the questions.

1. What examples of medications are mentioned that are based on rainforest remedies?
2. What is special about the new generation of painkillers being developed?

Remedies from the rainforest

In the botanically rich environment of the South American jungle, many indigenous Indian tribes have co-existed with nature harmoniously for a long time. During that time they have learned a great deal about the healing effects of various herbs of the rainforest. The healers or medicine men of each tribe are known as *Shamans*. Their knowledge has been passed down from generation to generation.

Scientists have become increasingly aware of the special knowledge that the Shamans have. This is why research teams from different universities are now working in close cooperation with tribal healers. Every day, more and more plants are being discovered. Scientists believe that there are more than 2,000 plants growing in the jungles of South America that can help in the fight against cancer. Yet they have tested only 1 per cent of the potentially healing plants that grow there. Who knows how many anti-ageing therapies and drugs might be derived from the remaining 99 per cent?

Some medications have already been successfully produced from rainforest plants. For decades, Quinine, made from the bark of cinchona trees, has been used to prevent millions of people around the world from dying of malaria. Or you may have heard of Curare, a herbal poison used by Indian hunters on their arrows when they go hunting. Today, the same chemical substance is the basis of medications for treating serious diseases such as Parkinson's disease.

Scientists have also reported that a new generation of painkillers is being developed, which are much more powerful than heroin, but are non-addictive. These painkillers, believe it or not, are based on a frog venom traditionally used by Amazon natives for *shamanic* purposes. Rainforest plants were being used by native Indians long before the Europeans arrived. Unfortunately, it has taken us nearly 500 years to realise the value of these ancient medicines!

6 Grammar

Passive continuous tenses

(a) Complete the sentences from the text. Then complete the rule.

1. Every day, more and more plants .... discovered.
2. A new generation of painkillers .... developed.
3. These plants .... used by native Indians long before the Europeans arrived.

> **Rule:**
> - We form the passive continuous form with the verb .... in the relevant tense, followed by *being* and then the ....

(b) Rewrite the sentences using the correct form of the passive continuous. Use the past participles in brackets to help you.

1. Scientists are doing a lot of research into plants from the Amazon. **(done)**
   A lot of research *is being done* into plants from the Amazon.
2. Many people are using plant medicines because they are often cheaper. **(used)**
   Plant medicines ....
3. Each year in the 1990s people were destroying an area of rainforest the size of Belgium. **(destroyed)**
   An area of rainforest .... each year in the 1990s.
4. People were making a lot of money from cutting down the Amazon. **(made)**
   A lot of money .... from cutting down the Amazon.
5. Holiday companies in Britain are now advertising eco-holidays on TV. **(advertised)**
   Eco-holidays ....
6. Every year, scientists are finding new types of plants in the rainforest. **(found)**
   Every year, new .... in the rainforest.

7 Listen

(a) 🔊 Listen to Andy and Cathy talking about flower remedies.
Match the remedies 1–6 with the problems a–f.

1	holly	a	feeling very sorry for yourself
2	larch	b	feeling very depressed, often with no real reason
3	mustard	c	feeling guilty about something
4	olive	d	having little or no confidence
5	pine	e	feeling exhausted after a lot of effort
6	willow	f	feeling jealous of other people; hating other people

(b) 🔊 Listen again and mark the statements T (true) or F (false).
Correct the false statements.

1 Andy is taking medicine because he's very tired. ☐
2 Andy doesn't believe in flower remedies. ☐
3 Flower remedies are more for curing the mind than the body. ☐
4 You take a flower remedy by adding drops to water. ☐
5 There are more than 40 flower remedies. ☐

Holly Larch

Mustard Olive

Pine Willow

8 Vocabulary

Feelings

(a) Match the adjectives 1–6 with the definitions a–f.

1	panicky	a	not paying attention
2	homesick	b	thinking a lot about the past and imagining that it was better than the present
3	inattentive	c	easily scared
4	absent-minded	d	wishing you were at home
5	over-anxious	e	tending to forget things because you are thinking about other things
6	nostalgic	f	too worried about something

(b) Complete the sentences with adjectives from Exercises 7a and 8a.

1 They must have taken the money, because they're looking so ....

2 He was so .... that he didn't notice that he'd left his umbrella on the bus.

3 We were so .... after our twelve-hour flight that we could hardly follow the conversation.

4 He had always been very .... of his brother's good looks.

5 He's scared of everything, even little spiders. Is he the .... type?

6 When I travel, if I get a bit .... , I just phone home. It's so easy these days.

7 Her children make a lot of noise in the garden, but she doesn't notice. She's completely ....

8 My parents are always talking about when they were young – they're so .... about the past.

9 Speak

(a) Work with a partner. Discuss the questions.

1 What do you think about flower remedies? Do you think they work?
2 Can you think of two friends or members of your family who have problems? How do they feel?
3 Which flower remedies do you think might help?

(b) Now discuss your ideas with another pair.

Eyes open

10 Read and listen

(a) 🔊 What kind of test has Ash got on Friday? What result does he get? Read, listen and check your answers.

Joanne: So when's your test, Ash?

Ash: Oh please – don't talk to me about that. I'm nervous enough as it is.

Matt: How come you're so nervous about it? Don't you think you'll pass?

Ash: Frankly, I'm convinced I won't. The test is on Friday. My instructor says I'm ready, but I can see myself failing and just throwing away all the money I've spent on lessons and the test.

Caroline: So – you need to see yourself passing. If you can do that, you're well on your way.

Joanne: What do you mean by that, Caroline?

Caroline: Well, it's interesting, isn't it, that Ash said 'I see myself failing'? It's a kind of visualisation. In your mind, you 'see' failure, and so that's probably–

Matt: You're off your trolley!

Caroline: Matt – let me finish, will you? If you 'see' failure, that's probably what you'll get. But maybe if you close your eyes and 'see' success, you'll get success.

Ash: Easier said than done!

Joanne: Well, it sounds interesting. Maybe you should try it.

Caroline: Yes. Positive thinking. It works. Try it, Ash. You might be surprised.

Ash: OK, I will. I'll try anything!

On Friday

Ash: So – did I pass?

Examiner: I'm afraid not. You failed on six different things. To be honest, Mr Taylor, sometimes I felt that you were driving with your eyes closed.

Later

Joanne: Hey Ash! That's a big smile you've got. I think we're going to hear some good news!

Matt: Yeah – you passed! Good on you, Ash!

Ash: Actually, I failed. Completely. The examiner said she'd never seen anyone quite so bad!

Caroline: Well, you don't seem too upset.

Ash: Well, you know, it wasn't such a bad day. When I was leaving, I saw this really good-looking girl waiting to do her test. And I thought: 'I'd really like to go out with her.' So I–

Joanne: But Ash, what's this got to do with anything–

Ash: Hang on a minute – I haven't finished. Anyway, I decided to do some positive thinking and I started to 'see' myself on a date with her.

Caroline: And?

Ash: And we're meeting up at eight o'clock tomorrow. We're driving over to Manchester for a meal.

Matt: Driving? How on earth can you be driving?

Ash: *She* passed!

(b) Read the text again. Answer the questions.

1 What result does Ash expect to get in his driving test?

2 What does Caroline suggest that Ash should do?

3 How many things did Ash fail his test on?

4 Where is Ash going tomorrow, and who with?

11 Everyday English

(a) Find expressions 1–5 in the story. Who says them?

1 how come ...?

2 how on earth ...?

3 easier said than done

4 you're well on your way

5 off your trolley

Which one is used to:

a express strong surprise? ☐

b ask for a reason? ☐

c say that you think someone is crazy? ☐

d encourage someone? ☐

e say that something is more difficult than you think? ☐

b Use one of the phrases in each space.

1 A: .... you're late again, James?

B: I'm sorry, my bus was delayed.

2 A: I'm so tired this morning.

B: Well, go to bed earlier, then you won't be tired.

A: .... I'm working on my project at the moment, and there's no way I can get to bed before 11.

3 A: Can you give me some money, Dad?

B: .... can you have no money left? I gave you £20 yesterday!

A: I know, but I had to buy a book for the literature exam.

4 A: This project is so much work. I haven't done half of it.

B: .... , really. I haven't even started yet!

c two examples of people interrupting in the story. How do they interrupt? What does the other person say?

12 Write

A guide to a happy life

What can you do to improve the quality of your life? Choose three areas and write a short paragraph for each one explaining your ideas.

The best answers will be published in the school magazine.

a You see this poster on the school notice board and decide to enter the competition. First brainstorm some ideas. Read the list below and add more ideas of your own.

watch what you eat
don't watch, participate
learn how to use your time well

help other people
learn how to do something well
talk about your problems

think positively about yourself
laugh a lot

b Read the paragraphs below quickly. Which of the brainstorming ideas above do they talk about?

People often don't do what they really want to because of a fear of failure. You don't apply for a job in case you don't get it. You don't perform at the school concert because others might laugh at you. A lack of confidence can cause a lot of misery.

The secret to overcoming this problem is learning to believe in yourself. This might be easier said than done, but there are many things to help you do this. Talk about your problem with a friend or look for advice on the internet. Visualise yourself being successful and practise breathing techniques to keep you calm when you get nervous. And the most important thing is: believe you can do it. When you've learned to do that, you're well on your way.

c Topic sentences are used at the beginning of a paragraph to introduce the ideas that are going to be expressed in it. Underline the two topic sentences in the text above.

d You can often make your writing more interesting by giving examples. Look back at the model text and underline the examples it contains.

e Now write two more paragraphs of your own for the competition.

  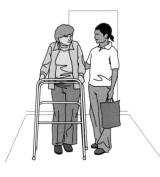 

3 Brainwaves

* Defining and non-defining relative clauses review
* Relative clauses: *which* referring back to an idea
* Vocabulary: sports

1 Read and listen

(a) Guess the answers to these questions. Then read the text to check.

1 Who looks longer at a face – newborn girls or newborn boys?
2 Who is generally better at noticing changes in people's feelings – men or women?

They just can't help it

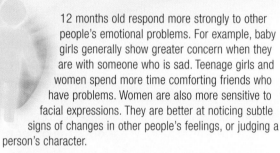

What kind of brain do you have? Simon Baron-Cohen, who has done intensive research, says there really are big differences between male and female brains.

My theory is that the female brain is mainly built for empathy (E) – the ability to understand other people – and that the male brain is mainly built for understanding and building systems (S). According to this theory, there are three brain types: the E-brain, the S-brain and the 'balanced brain' which has both abilities – empathy and systems-thinking (the ability to understand how things work).

It is important to stress that not all men have the S-brain, and not all women have the E-brain. But generally, there are clear differences. For example, women tend to choose different things to read on the railway platform or in the airport departure lounge. They are more likely to go for magazines on fashion, romance, beauty, counselling and parenting. Men are more likely to choose magazines that feature computers, cars, photography, DIY, sport and the outdoors.

You may think that these preferences are in some way influenced by people's upbringing. However, there is scientific evidence to suggest that this is not the case.

A new study carried out in the lab where I work at Cambridge University shows that newborn girls look longer at a face, and newborn boys look longer at a mechanical mobile, which suggests that certain differences between male and female brains are biological. It has also been observed that baby girls as young as

12 months old respond more strongly to other people's emotional problems. For example, baby girls generally show greater concern when they are with someone who is sad. Teenage girls and women spend more time comforting friends who have problems. Women are also more sensitive to facial expressions. They are better at noticing subtle signs of changes in other people's feelings, or judging a person's character.

Boys, from an early age onwards, seem to love putting things together, building toy towers or towns or vehicles. Boys also enjoy playing with toys which have clear functions, which have buttons to press, things that light up, or devices that will cause another object to move. You see the same sort of pattern in the adult workplace. People whose jobs are in metal-working or the construction industries are almost entirely male. Maths, physics and engineering, which require high levels of systems-thinking are also largely male-chosen disciplines.

Some people may worry that I am suggesting that one gender is better than the other, but this is not the case. The theory says that, on the whole, males and females differ in the kinds of things that they are interested in and that they find easy, but that both genders have their strengths and their weaknesses. Neither gender is superior overall.

Others may worry that a theory like this creates gender stereotypes, which is not true. The study simply looks at males and females as two groups, and asks what differences exist, and why they are there.

(b) Read the text again and listen. Answer the questions.

1 Which abilities are more related to the 'E-brain'?
2 What does the text say about boys and girls and what reason is given for these differences?
3 Why are some people critical of the theory?
4 What evidence is there to suggest that the differences in men and women's likes/dislikes are not just influenced by their upbringing?
5 What is your own opinion about the theory presented in the article?

2 Grammar

Relative clauses review

a) Use the text in Exercise 1 to complete these sentences.

1 Men are more likely to choose magazines _____ feature computers, cars, boats, photography, DIY, sport, hi-fi and the outdoors.

2 Teenage girls and women spend more time comforting friends _____ have problems.

3 A new study carried out in the lab _____ I work at Cambridge University shows that new-born girls look longer at a face.

4 Boys also enjoy playing with toys _____ have clear functions.

5 People _____ jobs are in metal-working or the construction industries are almost entirely male.

b) Complete the rule.

> **Rule:**
> * We use _____ to refer to people.
> * We use _____ or _____ to refer to things.
> * We use _____ to refer to places.
> * We use _____ to refer to possession.

c) Mark the sentences *D* or *A*.

D = the underlined part gives defining, important information about the person or thing(s).

A = the underlined part gives additional information about the person or thing(s).

1 Boys prefer subjects <u>which require thinking about systems</u>. *D*

2 Simon Baron-Cohen, <u>who has done intensive research</u>, says there are big differences between male and female brains. _____

3 Maths, physics, and engineering, <u>which require high levels of systems-thinking</u>, are also largely male-chosen disciplines. _____

4 We talked to a man <u>who has done intensive research</u> on this topic. _____

5 My brother, <u>whose office is in London</u>, has to travel an hour each way to and from work. _____

Look

Relative clauses with *which*

The pronoun *which* normally refers to a noun, but it can also sometimes refer to the whole of a previous clause.

what, *that* and *how* cannot be used in this way.

*Jo couldn't get a ticket, **which** was a pity.*

NOT ~~Jo couldn't get a ticket, what was a pity.~~

d) Look at the examples. In each case, what does *which* refer back to?

*A new study shows that new-born girls look longer at a face, and new-born boys look longer at a mechanical mobile, **which** suggests that certain differences between male and female brains are biological.*

*Other people may worry that the theory creates gender stereotypes, **which** is not true.*

e) Complete the second sentence so that it has a similar meaning to the first. Use *which*.

1 Because you can't talk to babies, it makes it difficult to do research about their minds.

You can't talk to babies, which makes it difficult to do research about their minds.

2 Some men and boys can be very aggressive, but this isn't true of so many girls and women.

Some _____ girls and women.

3 The research is controversial because it is about male and female brains.

The research is about _____ makes it controversial.

4 The fact that girls often notice people's problems means female brains may be built more for empathy.

Girls often _____ built for empathy.

5 Maths requires a lot of systems-thinking and that's why a lot of men choose it.

Maths _____ men choose it.

6 The author says that both genders have strengths and weaknesses and that makes a lot of sense.

The author _____ a lot of sense.

$$\Delta x = xf - x_0$$
$$\Delta t = t_2 - t_1$$
$$V = \Delta d / \Delta t$$

3 Speak and listen

a) Look at the pictures and say what the sports are. Then put them into three categories:

1 = have tried
2 = have never tried but would like to try
3 = have never tried and wouldn't like to try

Tennis

Football

Gymnastics

Car racing

Kick boxing

Skateboarding

Volleyball

Surfing

b) What other sports can you add to each list?

c) Work in pairs. Discuss your lists and give reasons for your choices.

d) You are going to hear information about two sportswomen, Danica Patrick (a racing car driver) and Maribel Dominguez (a football player). Who do you think says:

1 'I started out in go-karts.'
2 'In Mexico we don't have even a decent amateur league for women.'
3 'I haven't flipped a racing car.'
4 'Knock on wood, I haven't broken a bone.'
5 'To play in one of those tournaments feels just incredible.'
6 'I just really like to accomplish things.'
7 'There is nothing like it. It is beyond words.'

e) 🔊 Listen and check your answers.

f) Listen to the interview with Danica Patrick again and answer the questions.

1 How old was she when she started racing?
2 What is her philosophy about speed?
3 Why does she like ironing shirts?
4 What does this tell us about her motivation?

g) 🔊 Listen to the news item about Maribel Dominguez again and answer the questions.

1 Why did she find herself in the news?
2 Why did boys let her play football with them when she was young?
3 What are her ambitions for the future?
4 What does she think is the best thing about football for a) a woman and b) a man?

Discussion box

Work in pairs or small groups. Discuss these questions together.

1 Do you know of any women who made it or tried to make it in a male sport?
2 Do you think women and men should be allowed to compete in the same sports? Explain your reasons.

4 Vocabulary and speaking
Sports

a  Read the texts. What sports are the people talking about? Choose from the sports in the table in Exercise 4b. Listen and check.

1 'The sea was really rough and the waves were huge. I got knocked off my board a few times but it was great.'
_____surfing_____

2 'I took the ball past three of their defenders and then kicked the ball into the back of the net. All my team-mates ran across the pitch to celebrate with me. What a goal.' _____

3 'I love going down to the local rink to watch a game. The way those men move so quickly across the ice on their skates. And the control they have of the puck with their sticks. It's amazing. ' _____

4 'His glove hit me really hard in the face. I'm glad I was wearing a helmet. They had to carry me out of the ring.'
_____

5 'He hit the ball into the net. He was so angry that he threw his racket on the ground. All around the court the spectators started booing him.' _____

6 'It's my favourite sport. All you need is a cap and some goggles. There's a really good pool just down the road from my house. I go everyday. It's the complete exercise.'
_____

b Read the texts again and complete the table.

	equipment needed	place where it is done
tennis	_____	_____
football	_____	_____
ice-hockey	_____	_____
boxing	_____	_____
surfing	_____	_____
swimming	_____	_____

c Work in pairs. Take turns to choose a sport. Your partner has five _yes/no_ questions to guess it.

Do you need a ball? Is it a team sport? Do you play it inside?

d Complete the questions with the correct form of the words in the box.

win	score	get sent off
draw	beat	lose

1 How do you feel when your team _____ a match?

2 Have you ever _____ a medal or a cup in a sport?

3 How do you feel when your best friend _____ you at sport?

4 What do you think of footballers' celebrations after they _____ a goal?

5 How do you feel when a player of your team _____ by the referee?

6 In some sports (like basketball and baseball), a _____ is impossible – one team must win. Do you think this is a good idea?

e Work in groups. Discuss the questions above.

5 Pronunciation
Intonation in questions
 Turn to page 120.

Culture in mind

6 Read

(a) Look at the pictures. What is your idea of 'intelligence'? Which pictures do you most associate with 'intelligence', and which the least?

(b) Read the magazine article and answer the questions.

1. What general differences are there in the concept of intelligence between Western and non-Western cultures?
2. Which culture values the ability to hide your intelligence at certain times?
3. What skills are valued more than reading, writing and maths in Eastern cultures?

Discussion box

Work in pairs or small groups. Discuss these questions together.

1. How would you define intelligence?
2. Which do you think is more important, academic intelligence or social and interpersonal intelligence?

Intelligence across cultures

What is intelligence? Is it about being clever and getting A grades in all your school subjects? Or is it more complicated than that? Recent research in Asia, Africa and Latin America suggests that the concept of intelligence differs from culture to culture.

This research has shown that people in non-Western cultures often have ideas about intelligence that differ fundamentally from those in Western cultures. The studies show that people in Western cultures tend to see intelligence in terms of one's ability to solve problems and engage in rational debate. Meanwhile, Eastern cultures see intelligence in terms of people's ability to successfully play their roles within social hierarchies both at home and at work.

Researchers at the National Chi-Nan University in Taiwan found that Taiwanese-Chinese ideas of intelligence emphasise understanding and relating to others, including knowing when to show and when not to show one's intelligence.

In a study conducted in San Jose, California, immigrant parents from Cambodia, Mexico, the Philippines and Vietnam, as well as native-born Anglo-Americans and Mexican-Americans, were asked what they saw as important in the development of their children's intelligence. Parents from all groups – except Anglo-Americans – indicated that motivation and social skills were as important as, or more important than, academic skills in the development of their children.

Another study shows major differences in how much importance is given to verbal and non-verbal communication skills. Western cultures seem to value more highly the ability to say things clearly, whereas non-Western cultures seem to value the use and understanding of gestures and facial expressions.

Intelligence expert David Lazear says that in the Western world we tend to think that the most important thing about being smart is to have skills in reading, writing and mathematics. 'However, many Asian cultures place at least equal value on the development of one's interpersonal skills. These include being an effective team member, or the ability to create agreement within a group of people. Many Asian cultures also highly rate the development of a person's introspective abilities. This is the ability to "go inside" and acquire knowledge about yourself and then to be able to act on this increased self-knowledge. When I lived and worked in Africa, I found great importance given to such things as dance, music, art and drama as ways to express the deep wisdom of the culture and to reinforce key personal and social values. All the intelligences were valued, but somehow capacity in these areas was seen as special and even more profound.'

7 Write

(a) Read the composition quickly. Do you think the text was written by a girl or a boy? Give your reasons.

(b) Read the composition again and complete it with the words in the box.

> to conclude   moreover   however
> for example

(c) What is the purpose of each paragraph? Write A–D in the boxes.

A   the writer's conclusion

B   positive points

C   introducing the topic

D   negative points

(d) Write your own composition on a different sport. Use the steps below to help you.

- Think about the topic. Note down your ideas in a mind map.

fascinating game

aggression of fans

brings people together

injuries

The positives

The negatives

football

My opinions

in favour   good spectator sport

- Organise your ideas to fit into four paragraphs:

  Paragraph 1: introduce the topic

  Paragraph 2: positive points

  Paragraph 3: negative points

  Paragraph 4: your conclusion

- Write your composition. Use your notes to help you.

- If possible, have a break. Then check your writing and try to improve it, if you can.

[   ] Boxing is a popular sport that many people seem to be fascinated by. Newspapers, magazines and sports programmes on TV frequently cover boxing matches. Professional boxers earn a lot of money, and successful boxers are treated as big heroes.

[   ] It seems to me that some people, especially men, find it appealing because it is an aggressive sport. When they watch a boxing match, they can identify with the winning boxer, and this gives them the feeling of being a winner themselves. Sometimes fans are rooting for a particular boxer, [1] _____ because the boxer comes from their own country, and if 'their' boxer loses, they often feel as if they have lost a fight themselves. It is a fact that many people have feelings of aggression from time to time, but they cannot show their aggression in their everyday lives. Watching a boxing match gives them an outlet for this aggression.

[   ] [2] _____ , there is a negative side to boxing. It can be a very dangerous sport. Although boxers wear gloves during the fights, and amateur boxers even have to wear helmets, there have frequently been accidents in both professional and amateur boxing, sometimes with dramatic consequences. Boxers have suffered from head injuries, and, occasionally, fighters have even been killed as a result of being knocked out in the ring. [3] _____ , studies have shown that there are often long-term effects of boxing, in the form of serious brain damage, even if a boxer has never been knocked out.

[   ] [4] _____ , I am personally not at all in favour of aggressive sports like boxing. I think it would be better if less time was given to aggressive sports on TV, and we celebrated more men and women from non-aggressive sports as our heroes and heroines in our society. I believe that the world is aggressive enough already! Of course, people like competitive sports, and so do I, but I think that hitting other people in an aggressive way is not something that should be regarded as a sport.

4 Time travellers

* Reported speech review
* Vocabulary: time expressions
* Vocabulary: reporting verbs

1 Read and listen

(a) Read the extract from a TV guide. Have you ever seen this TV programme? (Circle) the correct words.

1 Doctor Who was last on TV in *1985 / 1989*.
2 Doctor Who is a *medical doctor / Time Lord*.
3 Doctor Who works *with an assistant / on his own*.
4 Doctor Who is a *film / TV series*.

(b) Listen and choose the correct answers.

Today's TV Sat 12th March 2005

After a 16 year absence, *Doctor Who* returns to our TV screens this Saturday. This time, the charismatic time-travelling Time Lord is played by Christopher Eccleston, while Billie Piper plays his enthusiastic sidekick Rose. Whether you're a fan of the original series or too young to remember it the first time around, don't miss the exciting rebirth of this cult classic.

1 When was the cult BBC TV series, *Doctor Who*, first broadcast?

a 1936 b 1956 c 1963 d 1999

2 What genre is the show?

a science fiction b comedy
c horror d a mixture of different genres

3 Why does the Doctor not respect the Time Lords' promise?

a Because he's evil.
b Because he wants to make the world a better place.
c Because he was sent away from the planet Gallifrey.
d Because he's bored and wants something to do.

4 Which of these is the Tardis?

5 What's special about the Tardis?

a It's very fast.
b It has a lot of weapons.
c It can disappear.
d It's bigger on the inside than it is on the outside.

6 Which of these is a Dalek?

7 How many actors have played Doctor Who?

a 7 b 8 c 9 d 10

8 Which best describes a Doctor Who assistant?

a A young woman from another planet.
b A young woman from Earth in the past.
c A young woman from Earth in the present.
d A young woman from Earth in the future.

2 Grammar

Reported speech review

a Write down what each person actually said.

1 William Hartnell said that his health was getting worse.

   'My health is getting worse.'

2 He said that he couldn't play the Doctor any more.

3 The woman said that she'd never heard of Doctor Who.

4 The Time Lords said that they would never change anything in the universe.

b What happens to the verb in reported speech when the reporting verb is in the past? Complete the table.

Direct speech	Reported speech
present simple →	...*past simple*...
present continuous →	-------------------------
present perfect →	-------------------------
past simple →	-------------------------
can / can't →	-------------------------
will / won't →	-------------------------
must →	-------------------------

c What other words change in reported speech?

d Write the reported speech.

1 'The Daleks are coming!' said the assistant.

   The assistant said that the Daleks were coming.

2 'We have to get to the Tardis before it's too late,' said the Doctor.

3 'We'll only know what year it is outside when we arrive,' said the Doctor.

4 'I've got a plan and I know how we can kill the Ice-men,' said the Doctor.

5 'You're getting the time wrong!' Romana told the Doctor.

6 'I've heard so much about you,' Chronotis told the Doctor.

7 'We don't know what is going on,' said the Doctor.

8 'There won't be enough time!' announced the Doctor.

3 Vocabulary

Expressions with *time*

◁)) ⟨Circle⟩ the correct option. Then listen and check.

1 Come on! Quickly! We're *taking / running* out of time!

2 My father's always busy. He never *wastes / has* time to relax.

3 I'm not in a hurry. *Take / Give* your time.

4 Our Maths teacher often complains that we *give / spend* him a hard time.

5 I got home just *in / off* time to miss the rain.

6 I'm not late. I'm exactly *off / on* time. Look at the clock.

7 Come on, let's get started – we've *spent / wasted* a lot of time already.

8 I think you should take time *off / on* and go on holiday. You've worked too hard.

9 Annie's a very relaxed person. She *gives / spends* a lot of time meditating.

4 Pronunciation

Schwa /ə/ *teacher*

◁)) Turn to page 120.

5 Speak

Work with a partner. Student B: Turn to page 122. Student A: Ask your partner the questions. You start.

1 Are you always on time for your lessons? If not, what excuse do you give?

2 When did you last have the feeling that you had wasted a lot of time?

3 If you could take time off next week, which day would it be? Why?

4 Have you ever given a teacher a hard time? What did you do?

6 Read

a Read Cathy's letter to her father. What do you learn about her father in the letter?

Hi Dad,

[1] You're probably thinking that I'm writing to say how disappointed I am. Well, I won't pretend I'm not disappointed that you didn't come to my birthday party. After all, you're not 18 every day, and you always tell me how special I am to you. But the party was great – so don't worry, I'm not writing to complain! But there is a reason I'm writing, and I really hope you can take the time (difficult, eh?) to read this carefully!

[2] Remember when I was 15, and I got really fed up with school, and I was thinking of dropping out and becoming a hairdresser? I've still got the letter you wrote me then, and I often read it. You warned me that I'd probably regret it later, and encouraged me to think very carefully before making any decisions. I did think carefully. Your letter persuaded me to stay in school, and I'm glad it did!

[3] So here's what I want to say: I'm worried that you're working too hard, Dad! I know what you do is important. I know you have a lot of responsibility, and I know a lot of other people depend on the work you do, but I am concerned. I've just read a great book called Time Shifting. It was almost written for you. I know you'll never find the time to read it, so I've decided to sum up the key points for you.

'HIGHLY RECOMMENDED' – DEEPAK CHOPRA

TIME SHIFTING

A revolutionary new approach to creating more time for your life

Stephan Rechtschaffen

[4] • The writer says that when people keep themselves busy all the time, it's usually for a reason – he claims they're often trying to avoid their real feelings. Even in their free time, people speed up – they watch TV, surf the internet, go to the gym, anything except get in touch with their real feelings.

[5] • He advises managers not to think about making money all the time. For people who are totally stressed out about money, taking a break might seem like they're losing money – and not what it should be, time to relax!

[6] • He recommends 'shifting time' on a regular basis – especially in times of real stress. In other words, he suggests taking breaks, and doing certain things really slowly – 'normal' things, like going for a walk for ten minutes, or standing up from the desk and breathing slowly for a few minutes, or even washing the dishes! (How's that for a suggestion???)

[7] • And here's what I like best – and you know what it's about, don't you, Dad? Yes, driving!!! It's about managers who leave home, get into their car, overtake as many other cars as possible, and drive as fast as they can to save a few minutes on their way to work, but end up arriving feeling angry and stressed. (Be honest – doesn't this sound familiar, Dad?) Well, the book encourages people to try something completely different: leaving home ten minutes earlier, and taking your time while you drive. Then driving – like a lot of other things – can become a pleasant thing to do.

[8] Thanks for reading this, Dad. Promise me you'll take the time to think about it! And please remember that a very special person once convinced me that we can never make decisions for the people we love, but it's a sign of love to tell them what we honestly think. This, Dad, is what I honestly think.

All my love,

Cathy

b Read the letter again. In which paragraphs can you find the following:

1 a warning?
2 a recommendation?
3 a piece of advice?
4 a piece of encouragement?
5 a claim?

Discussion box

Work in pairs or small groups. Discuss these questions together.

1 Have you ever written or received a letter giving advice? What was it about?

2 How do you think Cathy's dad reacted when he read this letter?

7 Grammar

Reporting verbs review

a Different reporting verbs have different patterns after them. Put these verbs into the tables. Find examples in the letter in Exercise 6 to help you.

| claim | encourage | recommend (x2) | advise | suggest (x2) | warn (x2) |

say	
....	
state	that ...
emphasise	
.... (someone)	
recommend	
....	that you do ...
....	
....	doing ...
deny	

....	
convince	
....	someone (not) to do ...
persuade	
....	
....	
promise (not)	to do ...
refuse	

Look

We can also say *promise (someone) that ...*

b Match sentences 1–8 with speech types a–h.

1 'No. I won't help you,' she said.
2 'I won't be late,' he said.
3 'My father has won over fifty golf competitions,' he said.
4 'You're going to get ill if you don't eat more healthily!' the doctor said.
5 'It's not true that I work too hard,' she said.
6 'Try the new French restaurant. It's excellent,' they said.
7 'I think you should take a break sometimes,' the doctor said.
8 'Come on, Steve, you can do it! Jump!' she said.

a a claim
b a promise
c a warning
d a refusal
e a denial
f encouragement
g a recommendation
h advice

c Report the sentences in Exercise 7b.

She refused to help me.

8 Speak and listen

a You're going to listen to a song called *If I Could Turn Back Time*. What do you think the song is about?

1 Someone who regrets something they did.
2 Someone who wants to be a time traveller.
3 Someone whose boyfriend/girlfriend is in another country where the time is different.

b 🔊 Listen to the song. Put the words in the correct places.

> blind   care   hurt   knife   proud   reach
> strong   used   weapons   world

c Match the words 1–5 in the song with the definitions a–e:

1 take back those words
2 wound
3 shattered
4 drove
5 swore

a broke into very small pieces
b pushed strongly
c made a strong promise
d apologise for the things I said
e create pain

d We use *like* in English to compare one thing with another to help describe it. This is called a simile. Find three similes in the song.

e Write your own similes using the words here or ideas of your own.

1 Happiness is like ....
2 Fear is like ....
3 Love is like ....
4 This morning I ran out of the house like ....
5 I was really hungry and I ate like ....
6 Exams make me feel like ....
7 The sun set over the sea like ....
8 The moon was in the sky like ....

Did you know ...?

Cher's full name is Cherilyn Sarkisian Liden Chiles. Her singing career began in the 1960s, when together with her then-husband Sonny Bono she formed the duo Sonny and Cher, and had big hits like *I Got You Babe*. She has also had a very successful acting career, with films like *Mask* and *Moonstruck* (with Nicolas Cage).

If I Could Turn Back Time by Cher

If I could turn back time,
If I could find a way, I'd take back those
words that hurt you and you'd stay.
I don't know why I did the things I did,
I don't know why I said the things I said.
Pride's like a ¹............... , it can cut deep inside.
Words are like ²............... , they wound sometimes.
I didn't really mean to hurt you, I didn't want to see
you go. I know I made you cry, but baby:

[Chorus:]

If I could turn back time, if I could find a way,
I'd take back those words that ³............... you,
And you'd stay.
If I could ⁴............... the stars, I'd give them all to you
Then you'd love me, love me like you ⁵............... to do.
If I could turn back time.

My ⁶............... was shattered, I was torn apart,
Like someone took a knife and drove it deep in my heart
You walked out that door, I swore that I didn't
⁷...............
But I lost everything, darling, then and there.
Too ⁸............... to tell you I was sorry,
Too ⁹............... to tell you I was wrong.
I know that I was ¹⁰............... , and ooh...

[Chorus]

If I could turn back time, if I could turn back time,
if I could turn back time – ooh baby
I didn't really mean to hurt you, I didn't want
to see you go. I know I made you cry.

[Chorus]

9 Write

a Read the letter and answer the questions.

1 Why hasn't Sally written before?
2 What is she thinking about now?
3 When does she want to stay?
4 What does she want Alex to do?

b The underlined expressions in the letter are very formal. Replace them with these less formal expressions. Write numbers in the boxes in the letter.

1 can you let me know
2 I'm sorry I haven't written
3 write soon
4 if it's OK with you if I come
5 the last time I was there

c You're going to write Alex's letter back to Sally. Look at the expressions below. For each pair, tick the one you think you're likely to use in the letter.

1 a I was extremely pleased to hear ...
  b It was great to hear ...

2 a Is it OK if ...?
  b Would it be acceptable if ...?

3 a I hope you see ...
  b I trust you will understand ...

4 a I must apologise for the fact that ...
  b I'm sorry that ...

5 a Of course we can put you up here.
  b Naturally we can let you have a room.

d Write Alex's letter. Give Sally the following information:

● you want to see her again
● she can stay with you
● you already have plans for the week she suggested
● you can't change the plans
● the week before or after is OK

Add any further information or ideas that you want to.

Dear Alex,

<u>I apologise for not having written</u> ☐ before. Unfortunately I haven't had a lot of time, I've been very busy with exams this month at school. I'm sure you know how I feel!

Anyway, things are better now and I'm starting to think about the summer holidays. It's been a long time since we last spent any time together, so I was wondering <u>if it would be convenient for you if I came</u> ☐ to see you and perhaps stay with you for a few days in August. You know how much I love the area where you live, too – perhaps we could go cycling again like we did <u>on my previous visit</u>. ☐

So, is the week of the 10th to the 15th of August OK for you? Please don't feel that you have to say yes, but of course I'm hoping you will. Either way, <u>could you inform me</u> ☐ as soon as possible? I don't want to be pushy, but I'll have to make travel arrangements before too long.

All the best, and <u>looking forward to hearing from you</u> ☐

Sally

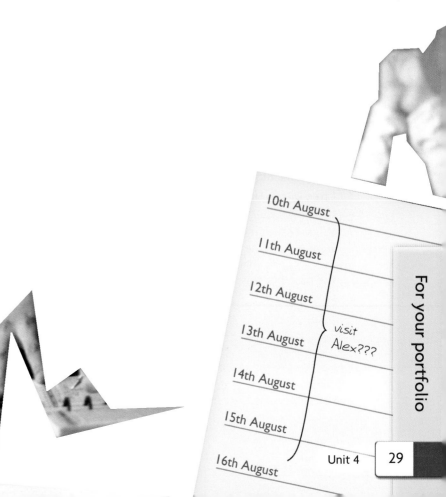

10th August
11th August
12th August
13th August | visit Alex???
14th August
15th August
16th August

Module 1 Check your progress

1 Grammar

(a) Use the correct form of the present simple or the present perfect simple to complete the sentences.

1 I _'ve_ just _read_ (read) an interesting article about the special abilities of 'autistic savants'.

2 Stephen Wiltshire _____ (paint) beautiful pictures since he was eight.

3 About 10% of children diagnosed with autism _____ (show) some special talent.

4 There's an Australian autistic savant, Daniel T, who speaks seven languages, and _____ even _____ (create) his own language.

5 Scientists _____ (study) Daniel's talents for some time with great fascination.

6 When he is not working, Daniel _____ (love) hanging out with friends.

[ ] 5

(b) Complete the sentences with the correct form of the past simple, past continuous or past perfect.

1 In 1857 Blind Tom _made_ (make) his first public appearance.

2 When Leslie L was born in the US in 1952, it soon turned out that he _____ (love) music and rhythm.

3 He _____ always _____ (sing) along to music that he heard on the radio.

4 Leslie _____ (start) playing Tchaikovsky's Piano Concerto No. 1, after hearing it only once before.

5 When Dustin Hoffman _____ (see) a programme about Leslie L on TV, he decided that he _____ (want) to play an autistic savant in a film.

6 Later, Dustin Hoffman's role of a savant in *Rainman* _____ (impress) many people.

7 When Leslie's mother died, some people were worried he would stop playing music, as _____ (happen) with other savants in the past, but this _____ (be) not the case.

[ ] 6

(c) Rewrite the sentences so that they are passive.

1 Researchers are doing various studies in order to understand the healing techniques of tribes.
Various studies are being done by researchers in order to understand the healing techniques of tribes.

2 Scientists have tested many rainforest plants for a cure for cancer.
Many rainforest plants _____

3 People are destroying huge areas of rainforest every day.
Huge areas of rainforest _____

4 Scientists are developing medication from frog poison.
Medication _____

5 Scientists have gained fascinating insights into some of the rainforests' secrets.
Fascinating insights _____

6 In the future, scientists will develop lots of new medications to help people with cancer.
Lots of new _____

7 A German scientist made aspirin into a modern medicine in 1897.
Aspirin _____

[ ] 6

(d) Connect the two sentences using the word at the end. You may need to take out a word in each sentence.

1 He told me that it was my mistake. It is nonsense. (which)
He told me that it was my mistake which is nonsense.

2 My friend wants to become a psychologist. She loves helping people. (who)

3 This is the book. Our teacher was talking about it. (which)

4 Many experts will attend the conference. New theories will be presented. (where)

5 I have recently read about a theory. It claims that differences between male and female brains can be explained through differences in their genes. (which)

6 Our neighbour is going to the UK soon. Her daughter lives in Portsmouth. (whose)

[ ] 5

e Rewrite the sentences using reported speech. Sometimes there is more than one possible answer.

1 Ken: *Doctor Who* is one of my favourite programmes. (said)

   Ken said that Doctor Who *was one of his favourite programmes.*

2 The aliens: we can destroy your planet. (claim)

3 The commander: Our spaceship will land soon. (warned)

4 My friend: I'll be at the club by five o'clock. (promised)

5 Steve: It's not true that I broke your mobile. (denied)

6 Our teacher: Repeat the phrases twice a day before the test. (recommended)

   [ ] 5

2 Vocabulary

a Complete the sentences with *mind*, *brain* or *time*.

1 It crossed my _mind_ yesterday that you must have a lot of work.

2 She always knows what I want to say before I say it. She seems to be able to read my _____ .

3 I know there was something else I wanted to do. But I can't remember – it's just slipped my _____ !

4 This homework is a bit difficult. Can I pick your _____ for a minute?

5 I don't know if I should buy this laptop. I'm in two _____ .

6 I got to the station just in _____ for the last train.

7 Mrs Jones will give you a hard _____ if you don't do your homework.

8 You're always reading that fashion magazine ... you've got clothes on the _____ !

   [ ] 7

b Complete the sentences with the words in the box. You may need to change the form.

| jealous   recover from   guilty   inattentive   doctor |
| diagnose with   ~~suffer~~   operating theatre |

1 After the accident she ___suffered___ from terrible headaches.

2 Soon after she came back from her holiday in Africa she was _____ malaria.

3 He's so _____ . He never knows what we're talking about.

4 She's so _____ . She can't stand it when other girls talk to James.

5 You don't need to feel _____ . I know it wasn't your mistake!

6 She had a serious operation, but she _____ it rather well.

7 The operation started at 9 o'clock. He was taken to the _____ an hour before that.

8 The _____ told him to drink plenty of water and rest in bed.

   [ ] 7

c Match the sentence halves to make sentences about sports.

1 She clearly was the best in her team. She

2 The player who had fouled the other goalkeeper

3 I hope it won't be a draw again since

4 She got knocked off the board a few times,

5 He was wearing a helmet, but was hit so hard

6 He was the best player on the rink. He's so

a got sent off by the referee.

b that he got knocked out in the first round.

c skilful with the puck.

d scored most of the goals.

e but she really enjoyed the strong wind.

f their last three games all ended 1:1.

   [ ] 6

How did you do?

Tick (✓) a box for each section.

Total score:	☺ Very good	☺ OK	☹ Not very good
[ ] 47			
Grammar	21 – 27	14 – 20	less than 14
Vocabulary	16 – 20	10 – 15	less than 10

Module 2
The way we are

YOU WILL LEARN ABOUT ...

- Famous people who had to live with shyness ....
- Objects that were all the rage for a while ....
- Flash mobs ....
- Birthday traditions in different countries ....
- Alfred Nobel and why he started an international award for peace ....
- Nobel Peace Prize winner Wangari Maathai ....

 Can you match each picture with a topic?

YOU WILL LEARN HOW TO ...

Speak
- Talk about personal qualities
- Discuss shyness
- Talk about the toys you played with as a child
- Organise a flash mob
- Talk about acts of kindness
- Talk about special presents you've received
- Talk about conflicts and how to resolve them

Write
- A description of a person
- A formal letter to a newspaper
- A summary
- A biography of a famous person

Read
- A questionnaire to find out how confident you are
- An extract from *Pride and Prejudice*
- An article on objects that were really fashionable for a while
- An article on a man who's trying to make the world a better place
- A website about birthday traditions
- An article on the origins of the Nobel Peace Prize

Listen
- An interview with an expert on shyness
- A news item on flash mobs
- An interview with someone who organises flash mobs
- People talking about special objects that they inherited
- An interview about a Nobel Peace Prize winner
- A song about *Peace, Love and Understanding*

Use grammar

Can you match the names of the grammar points with the examples?

What clauses	I **would** walk 3 miles to school every day.
Verbs with gerund or infinitive	He talked to me **in a friendly way**.
Talk about past habits	**It's hard** to say you're sorry sometimes.
Adverbial phrases	**What** I like about her **is that** she's really kind.
Dummy *it*	I **couldn't** see a thing.
The past perfect passive	I remembered **to phone** her.
The past perfect continuous	They **had been waiting** for three days.
A modal review	He **had been shot** three times.

Use vocabulary

Can you think of two more examples for each topic?

Personality adjectives	Verbs to do with conflicts	Childhood toys
honest	make up	dolls
funny	fall out	marbles
....	....	....
....	....	....

5 Personalities

* *what* clauses
* Verbs + gerund/infinitive review
* Vocabulary: personality

1 Read

a Read the questionnaire. How would you react in each situation?

Situation 1:

You're giving a presentation in your English class. You want to make a good impression on everyone. In the break before the presentation, you spill some coffee on your shirt.

a You're definitely not going to give a presentation with a stain on your shirt. You pretend that you are not feeling well and go home.

b You make a quick joke about the stain on your shirt, then forget about it and just concentrate on your presentation.

c You manage to cover up the coffee stain with your hand, but you feel awkward during the whole presentation. You're convinced that everyone thinks you look ridiculous.

Situation 2:

Your parents' friends have come for a visit, together with their teenage son/daughter who you quite like. Your father decides to show the photos of your last family holiday on the beach.

a You feel really embarrassed, but you look at the photos with the others. You don't say a word for the rest of the evening.

b While you're all looking at the photos you make loads of jokes and everyone finds your comments really funny.

c As soon as your father makes the suggestion, you get really angry. You make your father feel that the idea's silly and he gives up on it.

Situation 3:

A group of students from England is visiting your school and you have been asked to show them around. This means you will have to speak English. Then you hear that a local TV station wants to film the event.

a You think it's a great opportunity to practise your English. You know that you're going to make some mistakes, but you don't mind and can't wait to start.

b You agree, but you are worried that the event will be a real nightmare for you. On the day, your English is much worse than usual and you feel awful.

c As soon as you hear about the TV team, you refuse to show the students around.

Situation 4:

You are chatting on the internet with your friend. Suddenly your mum comes in and starts telling you off for not tidying your room. You completely forget about the microphone and get involved in a heated discussion with your mum. Your friend overhears the conversation. Later, you find out what happened.

a You explain the situation to your mum, and laugh about it together with her. You ask her if she has ever been in a similarly embarrassing situation.

b You are very angry with your mum and whenever you talk to your friend on the internet from now on you put up a sign on your door "Please don't come in. I'm busy!"

c You think the situation is so embarrassing that you do not talk to your mum for a week and avoid contact with your friend for quite some time.

Situation 5:

You are at school. You are very tired because you stayed up working on a project until late the previous night. Suddenly you fall asleep, and wake up to the loud laughter of the whole class and the teacher who have all noticed that you have been sleeping.

a You say that you're just practising your acting skills, and you must be very good at acting because they all believed it!

b You ignore the class' reaction, but the more you ignore it, the more you blush and the funnier your classmates think the situation is.

c You find the situation funny and laugh about it, apologise to the teacher and explain why you are so tired.

b Turn to page 122 to find your score. Do you agree with it?

2 Grammar

what clauses

a) Look at the examples. When do we use *that* to link the second part of the sentence?

What you need to realise is that no one ever comes across as being perfect all the time.

In five minutes no one will remember what happened.

This is what makes you come across as confident.

Look

Sometimes we use a comma instead of *that*.
What you need to realise is, no one is right all the time.

b) Join the sentences to make one.

1   John's really sensitive. I like this about him.
    What I like about John is that he's really sensitive.

2   He told me something. I don't remember it now.
    I don't remember _____

3   He never says 'please' or 'thank you'. This makes him seem rude.
    What makes _____

4   Everyone makes mistakes. You should remember this.
    What _____

5   He never stops talking. I find this really annoying.
    What _____

3 Vocabulary

Personality

a) Read about Bob's classmates. Tick (✓) the ones that you think he considers to be his friends.

1   Sue's *sympathetic*. She always listens to my problems and understands how I feel.

2   Charles is *charming*. He's good at making people like him and feel good about themselves.

3   Wendy's *witty*. She can always think quickly of something funny to say.

4   Cathy's *careless*. She does things too quickly and always makes mistakes.

5   Ian's *intellectual*. He loves learning about things.

6   Paul's *pushy*. He always wants me to do what he wants.

7   Simon's *shallow*. He doesn't care about anything.

8   Polly's *pretentious*. She tries to appear more important and clever than she is.

9   Sam's *smug*. He's always pleased with himself and satisfied about what he's achieved.

10 Barbara's *bubbly*. She's always happy, fun to be with, and energetic.

11 Chuck's *cheeky*. He shows a lack of respect, but often in a funny way.

12 Henry's *hypocritical*. He gives me advice, but he never follows it himself.

13 Steve's *scatty*. He's always forgetting and losing things.

b) ◁)) (Circle) the correct word. Listen and check.

1   All my friends were very *sympathetic / smug* when they heard about my accident. That helped me a lot.

2   Jane's really happy to be with James. She finds him quite *shallow / charming*.

3   I love reading, and my friends know it. They often say I'm the *scatty / intellectual* type.

4   She's really clever and she always gets the highest marks, but I wish she wasn't so *smug / witty* about it.

5   Don't be so *cheeky / careless* when you talk to her! She might not like your sense of humour.

6   We thought he was an interesting person, but when we spoke to him we found him rather *witty / shallow*.

7   She's rather *careless / pretentious* about her appearance — she always wears scruffy clothes.

8   I usually hate getting up, but my brother is different. He's always very *careless / bubbly* in the morning.

9   His speech made everyone laugh, and we all liked what he said. He's such a *witty / pushy* person!

10 He knows a great deal about art, but he's never *sympathetic / pretentious* about it.

11 The shop assistant was so *pushy / intellectual*. She tried to make us buy things we didn't want!

12 He's lost his keys for the third time this week! He's so *cheeky / scatty*.

13 He's the most *hypocritical / intellectual* person I know. He always tells others what they shouldn't eat, but he eats lots of junk food himself!

4 Pronunciation

Sentence stress and rhythm

🔊 Turn to page 120.

5 Speak

Work in small groups. Discuss the following.

1 Agree on four qualities you think are most important in a friend.

   A friend should be sympathetic.

2 For each quality, think of a famous person (a film star, singer, politician etc.) who you think has this quality.

3 Think about someone you have met. What was your first impression of them? Has your first impression changed since you got to know the person better?

   When I first met my brother's new girlfriend she came across as a bit shallow. But she isn't like that at all. Once you get to know her, you realise that she's a very interesting person, just a little shy.

6 Listen

(a) Look at the photos. Which of these people do you recognise? What do they do? What do they have in common?

(b) 🔊 Listen to this interview with the organiser of a self-help group and check your ideas.

(c) 🔊 In pairs, try to complete the summary in pencil. Then listen again and check.

Some people don't find it easy to talk to other people and they don't enjoy being in the ¹_____ , and they do everything they can in order not to be the centre of ²_____ . People are often not aware that shyness is quite a common phenomenon. Even some quite famous people are very shy.

Kim Basinger, who as a child never wanted to read aloud in front of the ³_____, found it hard to speak when she won an ⁴_____ .

Shyness is a kind of ⁵_____ anxiety. Shy people often think that others have a ⁶_____ opinion of them. But they can learn to ⁷_____ their shyness. Lots of people have done this, but we are unaware of this because when we ⁸_____ them, they have already overcome their shyness, and we don't see it any more. The first step is to accept that shyness is OK. However, sometimes shy people can give the wrong impression. Other people sometimes think they are a bit ⁹_____ or a bit ¹⁰_____ if they don't talk to them or ask them questions.

① ② ③

Discussion box

Work in pairs or small groups. Discuss these questions together.

1 What new information have you found out from the interview?

2 What are the disadvantages (or advantages) of being shy?

3 Do you think that it can be helpful for a person who is very shy to join a group like Monica's? Why / Why not?

4 Do you know any shy people? In what ways are they shy? Give examples of their behaviour.

7 Grammar

Verbs + gerund/infinitive review

a (Circle) the correct words in the sentences from the radio interview.

1 Not everyone enjoys *to be / being* in the spotlight.
2 Kim Basinger hated *to have / having* to read aloud in class.
3 Susie O'Neill preferred *not to be chosen / not being chosen* for team events.
4 She nearly stopped *to swim / swimming* altogether.
5 Bob Dylan couldn't stand *to go / going* on to the stage.
6 A lot of people refuse *to give in / giving in* to shyness.

b (Circle) the correct words.

> **Rule:**
> * The verbs *like, love, hate, prefer, begin* and *start* are usually followed by *a gerund / an infinitive*, but *a gerund / an infinitive* can also be used. There is no difference in meaning.
> * The verbs *enjoy, detest, don't mind, imagine, feel like, suggest, practise, miss* and *can't stand* must be followed by *a gerund / an infinitive*.
> * The verbs *refuse, hope, promise, ask, learn, expect, decide, afford, offer, choose* and *want* must be followed by *a gerund / an infinitive*.

c Look at these examples. What is the difference in meaning?

1a I stopped to drink my coffee   1b I stopped drinking my coffee.
2a I remember buying the book   2b I remembered to buy the book.

d (Circle) the correct word/s.

> **Rule:**
> * The verbs *stop* and *remember* can be followed by either a gerund or an infinitive but the meaning is *different / the same*.

try with infinitive or gerund

e Read the sentences from the radio interview. Then complete the rule. Write *gerund* or *infinitive*.

*Some people try **not to be** the centre of attention.*

*She tried **practising** her speech, but it didn't work.*

*Susie O'Neill almost tried **not to win**.*

> **Rule:**
> * We use *try* + ... to say that somebody does something to see what will happen.
> * We use *try* + ... to say that somebody makes an effort to do something.

f Match the sentences with the pictures.

1 We tried opening the window, but it was still really hot in the room. ☐
2 I tried to open the window, but it was stuck. ☐

g Complete the sentences with the verbs in brackets. Use the gerund or infinitive + *to*.

1 I can't stop .... (watch) this programme. It's brilliant.
2 I think they're really nice people, so I try .... (help) them as much as I can.
3 He's really charming. Please remember .... (invite) him.
4 I can't remember .... (see) that film.
5 We tried .... (surf) the internet, but we didn't find any information.
6 I met Oliver in town yesterday, so I stopped .... (talk) to him.
7 I remember .... (be) quite shy when I was little.
8 I thought she was very self-centred, so I stopped .... (go) around with her.
9 I tried .... (phone) you but my mobile was broken.
10 Please remember .... (give) me my book back tomorrow.

Literature in mind

8 Read

a Look at the cover of the book and read the short summary of the story. Would you be interested in reading the book? Why / Why not?

Pride and Prejudice

By Jane Austen

Pride and Prejudice *is about the Bennet family and their five daughters. Mrs Bennet wants to see them married, if possible to husbands who are better off than the family themselves. One of the daughters, Elizabeth, is not at all impressed by Mr Darcy when he doesn't give her a lot of attention at a dance. She considers him proud and arrogant. However, as this enchanting story of love, marriage and mutual understanding unfolds, Elizabeth finds out that a man can change his manners, and a lady can change her mind.*

b Read the story quickly and answer the questions.

1 Where does the scene take place?
2 What is the relationship between Mr Bingley and Mr Darcy?

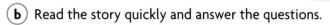

Mr. Bingley soon made himself acquainted with all the important people in the room; he was lively and unreserved, danced every dance, was angry that the ball finished so early, and talked of giving one himself at Netherfield. Such friendly qualities speak for themselves.

What a contrast between him and his friend! Mr. Darcy danced only once with Mrs. Hurst and once with Miss Bingley, declined to be introduced to any other lady, and spent the rest of the evening walking about the room, speaking occasionally to one of his own group. His character was decided. He was the proudest, most disagreeable man in the world, and everybody hoped that he would never come there again. Amongst the most violent against him was Mrs. Bennet, whose dislike of his general behaviour was sharpened because he had offended one of her daughters.

Elizabeth Bennet had been obliged, because there were very few gentlemen, to sit out two dances; and during part of that time, Mr. Darcy had been standing near enough for her to hear a conversation between him and Mr. Bingley, who came from the dance for a few minutes, to press his friend to join it.

'Come on, Darcy,' he said, 'you have to dance. I hate to see you standing about by yourself in this stupid manner. You really should dance.'

'I certainly won't. You know I hate it, unless I know my partner very well. At such an assembly as this it would be insupportable. Your sisters are with someone else, and there is no other woman in the room whom it would not be a punishment to me to dance with.'

'I wouldn't be as choosy as you are!' said Mr. Bingley. 'Honestly, I've never met so many pleasant girls in my life as I have this evening; and there are several of them who are unusually pretty.'

'You are dancing with the only pretty girl in the room,' said Mr. Darcy, looking at the eldest Miss Bennet.

'Oh! She's the most beautiful creature I've ever seen! But one of her sisters is sitting just behind you, she's very pretty, and probably very pleasant. Please let me ask my partner to introduce you.'

'Which one do you mean?' said Darcy, and turning round, he looked for a moment at Elizabeth, until their eyes met, and then he looked away and coldly said: 'She is tolerable, but not pretty enough to tempt *me*. I am in no mood right now to pay attention to young ladies who are ignored by other men. You'd better return to your partner and enjoy her smiles, for you are wasting your time with me.'

Mr. Bingley followed his advice. Mr. Darcy walked off; and Elizabeth remained without any very kind feelings toward him. She told the story, however, with great spirit among her friends; for she had a lively, playful disposition, which delighted in anything ridiculous.

c Read the story again and answer the questions.

1 Why did everyone hope that Mr Darcy 'would never come again'?

2 Why did Mrs Bennet especially dislike him?

3 What was Mr Darcy's reaction when Mr Bingley suggested to him that he should dance?

4 Why did Elizabeth overhear the conversation between Mr Bingley and Mr Darcy?

5 What reasons did Mr Darcy give for not wanting to dance with Elizabeth?

6 Why did Elizabeth tell her friends what Mr Darcy had said about her?

9 Write

a Put the adjectives in the box into two lists: personality and appearance. If necessary, use a dictionary to help you.

> sensible   disorganised   smart   tall
> cheerful   handsome   wavy   plump
> honest   slim   scruffy   lazy

b Can you add four more words to each list? Compare lists with a partner.

c Read the email. What does Jean talk about in the:

first paragraph?
second paragraph?
third paragraph?
fourth paragraph?

d When we write a physical description, we don't need to mention everything, just the most interesting parts. Look back at the third paragraph. Which two sentences could we leave out?

e How does Jean describe Bob's eyes and smile? Write similar descriptions of someone's:

1 hair   2 mouth

f When we describe someone's personality we often give examples of the person's behaviour to illustrate their qualities. Look back at paragraph four and find two examples of this.

8 Write a short description of someone who is:

1 generous

2 imaginative

Give examples of their behaviour to illustrate.

h Now write an email to a friend and tell them about a person you've recently met.

Hi Dawn,

(1) You missed a great party on Friday. Everyone was there, and we all missed you so much. The food was great and the music was brilliant. I don't think I've ever danced so much in my life.

(2) Anyway, let me give you the gossip before anyone else does. I met a really interesting guy at the party. His name's Bob and he's from Toronto. I've never met a Canadian before. He's in his last year at school and he's over here visiting his cousin for the summer holidays.

(3) But let me get to the interesting part. Bob must be the best-looking guy I've ever met. I mean he's gorgeous. He's average height too. The first thing that caught my attention were his amazing blue eyes. They're bright blue, like the colour of the ocean you see in those holiday postcards. I'm not exaggerating, honestly. His nose is quite small. He's got a great smile too. It's warm and friendly and you can't help liking him immediately when he smiles at you.

(4) But of course, the most important thing is that he's a very nice guy too. He's a very charming person and he made me feel good about myself. He said loads of nice things about me, which is always going to help you like someone, isn't it? But he's not just one of these guys who says things without meaning them. He came across as really being interested in me. I told him all about my problems with Betty and he really listened. He was so sympathetic and he gave me some good advice too. Now, you don't meet a guy who listens like that every day.

(5) Well, the bad news is that he's going back to Canada next week and I don't think I'll see him again. We said we'd email but you know how these things go. Never mind. It was just nice to have met someone so kind. Give me a call later.

Love Jean.

6 In and out of fashion

* Adverbial phrases
* *used to* and *would*
* Vocabulary: adverbial phrases

1 Read and listen

(a) What can you see in the photos? Have you ever played with any of these things?

(b) Read the texts quickly. What do you think is the main topic?

1 The three objects were a lot more expensive than they should have been.

2 The objects were bought by children, but also by adults in many countries.

3 Each of the objects was, at some time, the latest fashion and swept the world.

(c) 🔊 Read the texts again and listen. Write *hula hoop*, *Rubik Cube* or *Tamagotchi* next to the sentences below.

1 It was invented by a Hungarian.

2 Some people paid lots of money to get one.

3 Some people felt their toy had real needs.

4 Its inventors created another craze.

(d) Read the texts again. Underline the words that mean:

1 an activity, object or idea that is extremely popular, usually for a short time (text 1)

2 became popular (text 1)

3 became heavily involved in (text 1)

4 uncontrollable (text 2)

5 so pleasurable that you cannot stop doing it (text 2)

6 the most recent or modern (text 3)

7 amazing (text 3)

8 illegally (text 3)

1 The Hula Hoop

In 1957, a chance meeting between Americans Arthur Melin and Richard Knerr and an Australian, who was on holiday in California, resulted in one of the biggest crazes ever to sweep through the world. The Australian told them how children back home would twirl bamboo hoops around their waists in gym class for exercise. Melin and Knerr had an idea.

They started producing plastic hoops and introduced them to Californians. They caught on immediately; first with children and then, surprisingly, with adults too. It was only a matter of time before the rest of the US got caught up in the trend, and 25 million hula hoops were sold in two months. The fashion quickly spread overseas, with almost 100 million international orders in the first year.

However, not every country thought they were such a great idea. Some countries banned the hoop for 'moral reasons', others thought it was an example of the 'emptiness of American culture'. The hula hoop craze was short-lived, but the two entrepreneurs were already onto another hot idea – a small round disc of plastic which they called the frisbee.

Discussion box

Work in pairs or small groups. Discuss these questions together.

1 What other crazes can you think of in recent years?

2 What do you think made each of the toys so popular?

3 What do you think determines whether a new idea becomes a craze or not?

2 Rubik's Cube

There is only one solution and millions of ways of going wrong when it comes to solving 'The Cube'. One eighth of the world's population has laid hands on it, and more than 300 million of the most popular puzzles in history have been sold worldwide.

When Hungarian Erno Rubik first made his colourful cube in 1974, and showed it to some of his friends, the effect was instantaneous. Once they started fiddling excitedly with the Cube, they were hooked as they tried to get it back to its original position. The compulsive interest of friends and students in the Cube caught its creator by surprise, and it was months before any thought was given to the possibility of mass production.

However, a few years later, it seemed that the whole world was suddenly working away at their Cubes. People would play with them at home and at work, on buses, on tubes and in trains, in restaurants and in cafes. Everywhere you looked, someone had a Cube. As soon as you started playing with it, you couldn't put it down – the Cube was just too addictive.

3 Tamagotchis

Aki Maita used to be a housewife until she invented Tamagotchis. Suddenly, she was a multimillionaire. These plastic digital pets were launched in November 1996 and, within weeks, they had become the latest fashion. Demand for them was overwhelming. People used to patiently queue up in front of stores for hours to get one, and often prices paid on the black market would be ten times the shop price. Within a short period of time, millions of them had been sold in Japan and around the rest of the world. Some Japanese schoolgirls got mugged for their Tamagotchis, and businessmen would temporarily suspend meetings so that they could feed their pets. 'For some people, it was more than a toy, it was a learning device,' a psychologist said. 'It taught people to be responsible; to care for something like a pet, since people would try to extend the lives of their Tamagotchi pets as long as possible. They just could not ignore their Tamagotchi when it needed them.'

2 Speak

(a) Work in small groups. Choose one of the objects from the reading texts in Exercise 1. Imagine your job is to re-market this item to today's teenagers. Discuss the following:

1 What changes are you going to make to it so that it will appeal to a modern audience?
2 How are you going to advertise it?

(b) Present your ideas to the rest of the class. Which group has the best ideas?

3 Grammar

would and *used to*

(a) Complete the sentences from the text.

Habits and repeated actions

1 People .... play with them at home and at work.
2 People .... queue up in front of stores for hours to get a Tamagotchi.

States

3 Aki Maita .... be a housewife until she invented Tamagotchis.

(b) Complete the rule with *used to* and *would*.

> **Rule:**
> - When we talk about *habits* and *repeated actions* in the past we can use .... or ....
> - If we talk about a *permanent state* or *situation* (with verbs such as *be / think / love / have / want* etc.) we can only use ....

(c) Look at the sentences. ~~Cross out~~ *would* when it is not possible to use it.

1 I ~~would~~ / used to have a Tamagotchi.
2 I would / used to love it a lot.
3 I would / used to feed it every morning.
4 I would / used to sing it to sleep at night.
5 I would / used to think it was my best friend.
6 I would / used to take it everywhere I went.
7 I would / used to want nothing else.
8 I would / used to play with it for hours.

(d) Work with a partner. Talk about the toys in your childhood. Use *would* and *used to*.

I used to spend hours playing with ...
When I was young, I would ...

4 Listen

a Look at the photos. What do you think is happening in each photo? What do you think they might have in common?

b 🔊 Listen and check your ideas.

c 🔊 Mark the sentences *T* (true) or *F* (false). Correct the false statements.

1 The rug in the store cost $10,000.
2 The shop assistants reacted angrily to the flash mob.
3 The crowd stayed for fifteen minutes.
4 The people who lay down in the square didn't know each other.
5 The subway station in San Francisco was very busy.
6 The flash mob clapped loudly as people came out.
7 The man who started flash mobs is British.

d Imagine you are going to interview 'Bill'. What questions would you like to ask him? Write them down.

e Compare questions with a partner.

f 🔊 Listen to Bill. Which of your questions (if any) does he answer?

g 🔊 Listen again and answer these questions.

1 Why did Bill want to remain anonymous?
2 What happened in the flash mob in Rome?
3 What happened in the flash mob in London?
4 What are the two important things about flash mobs?
5 What did the British sociologist say about flash mobs?
6 What does Bill think about the future of flash mobs?

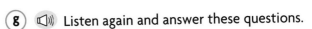

Discussion box

Work in pairs or small groups. Discuss these questions together.

1 Which of the flash mobs do you think is the most amusing?
2 If you could take part in a flash mob, would you? Why (not)?
3 Do you think there will be more flash mobs in the future?

5 Speak

a Work in small groups. Think of a fun flash mob event. Remember that:

- the event must not hurt anyone or be illegal!
- it should only last for a short time.

b Compare ideas with other groups. Which do you think is the best?

6 Grammar

Adverbs and adverbial phrases

(a) Complete the sentences with the words in the box.

> sudden   suddenly

About a hundred people _____ appeared.

There was a _____ movement.

(b) Complete the rule. Write *adverbs* or *adjectives*.

> **Rule:**
> - We use _____ to add information to nouns.
> - We use _____ to add information to verbs.

(c) We can also use *adverbial phrases* to say how someone does something. (A phrase is three or four words together.) Look at the adverbial phrases below. What types of words do we use with the expressions in A? What types of words do we use with the expressions in B?

(d) Add the words in the box to the lists below.

> difficulty   excitement   exciting
> horrible   interest   different

A

in a friendly *way*

in an interesting *way*

in a fun *way*

in an _____ *way*

in a _____ *way*

in a _____ *way*

B

with surprise

with enthusiasm

with fear

with _____

with _____

with _____

(e) Complete the sentences with the expressions from Exercise 6d. (There is often more than one possibility.)

1 It was a fantastic match – I was jumping up and down with
   _____excitement or enthusiasm._____

2 She seemed very nice – she smiled at me in _____

3 The homework was very hard – I only finished it with
   _____

4 The documentary was fascinating – I watched it with _____

5 In the film, I got scared when the woman screamed with _____

6 Anything is more enjoyable if you do it in _____

7 They come from a different part of the country, so they speak in
   _____

8 I love parties, so I replied to the invitation with
   _____

Aaaargh!

7 Vocabulary

Common adverbial phrases

(a) Match phrases 1–8 with definitions a–h.

1 by accident   a so that other people cannot hear
2 in a hurry   b one thing happening after another
3 in private   c intentionally
4 in public   d without telling other people
5 in secret   e not intentionally
6 in a row   f needing to do something quickly
7 on purpose   g without thinking properly
8 in a panic   h so that other people can hear

(b) Complete the sentences with the expressions in Exercise 7a.

1 It wasn't an accident – I think he did it _____ .

2 They organised the surprise party _____ , so I knew nothing about it.

3 We've won the competition five years _____ .

4 Could you go away, please, Jack? I want to talk to Sol
   _____ .

5 I'm really sorry – I broke your camera _____ .

6 My homework isn't very good. I did it _____ .

7 Please don't talk about my personal life _____ !

8 A fire broke out in the hotel and everybody ran out
   _____ .

8 Pronunciation

/æ/ *apple* and /e/ *lemon*

🔊 Turn to page 120.

Sorry!

9 Read and listen

a 🔊 What are Matt and Ash giving Joanne? Why? Read, listen and check your answers.

Caroline: What's the matter, Joanne? You don't look very happy at all.

Joanne: I'm not, but don't worry about it.

Matt: Is it anything we can help with?

Joanne: Probably not. You'll just think I'm being silly.

Ash: Try us, Joanne.

Joanne: Well, alright. It's just that I got home from school yesterday and I found that my mum had thrown out my teddy bear.

Matt: What! You've still got a teddy bear?

Caroline: Yeah, so? What's wrong with that?

Ash: Why did she throw it away?

Joanne: She said it was just lying there in my wardrobe taking up space and getting dirty.

Ash: You mean, you never even 'played' with it anyway? So she did have a point!

Joanne: Listen – it was part of my childhood, it had lots of memories for me. Oh, you wouldn't understand.

Caroline: Well, I do understand. I think it was really mean of her.

Matt: Well, I don't see the big deal. I mean you're eighteen, not eight.

Ash: We all have to grow up some time, Jo.

Joanne: Yeah, well, thanks for your support. I'll see you later.
(*She leaves the room*)

Caroline: You know, perhaps it's time you two grew up. You can be real idiots when you want to be.

Ash: What did we do?

Caroline: You made jokes when they weren't wanted, you weren't sympathetic, you failed to help a friend ... do you want me to go on?

Matt: What do you think we should do?

Caroline: Well, for a start, you could try and be more understanding.

The next day

Ash: Hi, Joanne.

Joanne: Oh, it's you two.

Matt: Yeah, listen. We're really sorry about yesterday. What we said was out of order.

Joanne: Well, don't worry about it.

Ash: Well we did worry, which is why we've got you this.

Joanne: Wow. It's lovely!

Matt: Do you like it?

Joanne: Well, it's not Miss Pinky, but it's the thought that counts. Besides, my mum's going to love it.

Ash: What? You called your teddy bear Miss Pinky!?

Joanne: Careful! I'm still thinking about whether I should forgive you or not.

b Read the text again. Answer the questions.

1 Why is Joanne reluctant to tell her friends what the matter is?

2 What reasons did Joanne's mum give for throwing her teddy bear away?

3 How does Caroline feel about Matt and Ash's reaction to Joanne's story? Why?

4 Why does Joanne say 'It's not Miss Pinky, but it's the thought that counts'?

10 Everyday English

a Find expressions 1–4 in the text. Who says them?

1 You can be <u>real</u> idiots when you want to be.

2 Well, <u>for a start</u>, you could try and be more understanding.

3 What we said was <u>out of order</u>.

4 <u>Besides</u>, my mum's going to love it.

Which one:

a is used to add another thought/idea? ☐

b means 'here's the first and most important thought/idea'? ☐

c is used to make the meaning of a noun much stronger? ☐

d means 'not suitable for the situation'? ☐

Letters to the editor...

(b) Complete the sentences with an expression from Exercise 10a.

1. A: Coming to the cinema with us?
   B: I can't, I've got homework to do. .... , I've run out of money!

2. A: I'm sorry about what I did yesterday.
   B: Well, you *should* be sorry – you were .... !

3. A: Can I help you with anything, mum?
   B: Well, yes – .... , you could tidy your room!

4. A: Did the exam go well?
   B: No, it didn't – in fact, it was a .... disaster!

11 Write

(a) Read letter a sent to a newspaper.

1. What is Mr Hill's opinion of flash mobbing?
2. What does the person who wrote the notes think of the letter?

(b) Read letter b. Which of the notes in letter a does the writer include in their letter?

(c) Read letter c. Underline the main points. Decide whether you agree or disagree with each of them. Make notes. Then write a reply to the editor.

(a)

1. This claim itself is ridiculous – no reason given!

2. Don't people have the right to decide for themselves?

3. What an intolerant view!

4. Yes, you are!

Dear Sir

The claim that flash mobs are art is clearly ridiculous, and can easily be dismissed. However, we should stop for a minute and ask ourselves if flash mobs shouldn't be forbidden altogether. Do people have nothing better to do than waste their time turning up in dozens at a sofa shop and asking for 'sunflowers in the rain', as customers and shopkeepers in one shop in the West End recently witnessed? Maybe I'm being old-fashioned, but I think that flash mobbing is not only a waste of time, it is also potentially dangerous. What if someone gets scared by a flash mob one day, over-reacts, and then the whole thing turns into a mini-riot? Surely no one will claim then that is art.

Yours sincerely
Mr Robert Hill

5. In fact this letter is potentially misleading, as it might make people believe that flash mobs are a bad thing!

(b) Dear Sir,

I am writing with regard to the letter in your newspaper concerning the flash mobs. I am concerned about the biased tone of the letter, and I would like to express my disagreement with it.

To begin with, the writer, without giving any reasons whatsoever, dismisses the idea that flash mobbing could be art. This in itself is a ridiculous view which I cannot share at all. Flash mobbing is a perfect example of playfulness and creativity, and I am grateful that there are people who put time into coming up with something provocative and 'useless'.

The writer also argues that flash mobs are a waste of time. Although nobody should have to take part in flash mobs unless they want to, we must accept that people have the right to decide for themselves how to use their time. The writer's position is not only extremely old-fashioned, it is narrow-minded. Whereas I see no potential danger in people coming together for a few minutes in public places to have fun and make others think, I see a lot of 'danger' in leading people to believe that flash mobs are something to be afraid of. I can only say – beware of such unfair and narrow-minded views!

(c) Dear Sir,

The tendency of young people today to give in to the marketing pressures of commerce and industry, and to buy whatever companies want them to buy, is saddening. Whether it is mobile phones, MP3 players, the latest fashion or, dare I say it, the internet – aren't all these things just crazes that cost a lot of money and are bad for young people today? When we were young, things used to be different. We had time for each other, we would go for walks and enjoy nature, and we would spend hours reading good books. How is the world going to develop if the only things young people are interested in are fads and electronic communication?

All I can say is that I'm deeply concerned, and I hope teachers are aware of the dangers of technology and the modern world, and influence children to turn more towards the things that really matter!

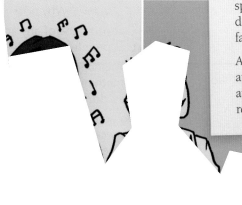

For your portfolio

Unit 6   45

7 Kindness matters

* Dummy *it*
* Modals review
* Vocabulary: ways of helping

1 Read and listen

a Who are the people and what are they doing? Read the text quickly to check your answer.

Hit-and-run kindness

(1) When Danny Wallace, 26, got bored, he put an advert on the worldwide web reading simply: 'Join Me. Send a passport photo.' A year and a half later his east London flat is the headquarters for a global internet-based 'club' whose members carry out good deeds for strangers every Friday.

(2) 'It's not common for people in London to talk to strangers. If you see someone <u>struggling</u> with something, part of your brain goes "I want to help". But the trained part of the brain says: "They will think you are mad or going to mug them", so you walk away.

(3) 'Join Me now has about 3,000 members around the world who do an act of kindness every Friday. For example, I'm usually out on a Friday so I go for one of the standard acts – the unexpected cup of coffee. You might be sitting in a café and see an old man in the corner drinking coffee or tea, and you walk up with another cup of whatever they are drinking, and say: "I've bought you a coffee" and walk away. It's a pleasure to see the look of surprise on their faces. There can be some suspicion, but I think that was mostly in the early days when I didn't know how to <u>do it properly</u>. I would walk up quite nervously like I was <u>doing something wrong</u> and I didn't know when to leave. In the

end, I learned through <u>trial and error</u>. Sometimes it worked, other times it didn't. I discovered that you have to walk up with confidence and humour and not "get in their faces". You say: "This is for you", then you go. It's hit-and-run kindness. And there is no point in doing it <u>half-heartedly</u>. You've got to do it because you really mean it.

(4) 'Join Me is without geographical boundaries, but there are quite a few members in London, and I get quite a lot of stories about things they have done on the Underground or on the buses. One lady got on the bus and put a £10 note down and said: "That's for me and the next nine people" so at every stop, anyone who got on was told it was paid for. A lot of people were doing this sort of thing anyway and <u>go to great lengths</u> to tell me. They <u>get a lot out of it</u>; for them it's an excuse or reason to do something nice for a complete stranger, and it gives them the confidence to walk up and start chatting. I think in London it is too easy to keep your head down. If people step on your foot on the Underground, they are an inch away but they won't say sorry because they don't want to speak out. Join Me helps you be a bit more confident and then you <u>find it easy</u> to ignore that social barrier.'

b 🔊 Read the text again and listen. Match topics A–D with paragraphs 1–4.

A *Join Me* encourages people to be kind to strangers. ☐

B People in London often don't stop to help strangers. ☐

C *Join Me* – How it started. ☐

D *Join Me* gives people more confidence. ☐

c Answer the questions.

1 What did Danny Wallace do one day and why?

2 How do Londoners often behave when they see someone in trouble?

3 What is special about members of *Join Me*?

4 Where in the world can one find people who belong to *Join Me*?

5 What do people like about being a member of *Join Me*?

Discussion box

Work in pairs or small groups. Discuss these questions together.

1 Would you become a member of *Join Me*? Why / Why not?

2 Can you think of any acts of kindness that people in *Join Me* could do?

3 Remember a time when someone did something kind for you. What did they do? How did you feel?

4 Do you believe that if you are kind to someone, then something good will happen to you? Can you think of any examples when this has happened?

2 Grammar

Dummy *it*

(a) Use the text in Exercise 1 to complete these sentences.

1 .... not common in London for people .... talk to strangers. (paragraph 2)

2 .... a pleasure .... see the look of surprise on their faces. (paragraph 3)

3 .... too easy .... keep your head down. (paragraph 4)

(b) Match the two parts of the sentences to make statements that you agree with. Compare answers with a partner.

1	It's nice to	see people who are unhappy.
2	It's easy to	ignore other people.
3	It's important to	be kind.
4	It's not unusual to	feel lonely.
5	It's wonderful to	understand why people don't talk to each other.
6	It hurts to	help people who need it.
7	It doesn't cost anything to	say you're sorry.
8	It feels good to	see people smile.

(c) Re-write the sentences, using *It ... to* to begin each sentence.

1 <u>Living</u> in the city is <u>great</u>. *It's great to live in the city.*

2 <u>Being</u> kind to people is <u>fun</u>. ....

3 <u>Helping</u> other people is <u>important</u>! ....

4 <u>Giving</u> money away to people on a bus? That's <u>crazy</u>! ....

5 Sometimes you <u>get</u> nervous. That's <u>normal</u>. ....

6 <u>Remembering</u> to say nice things isn't <u>hard</u>. ....

(d) Think about the place where <u>you</u> live. Write true sentences with the structure '*It ... to ...*'.

Where I live, it's difficult to get from one place to another.

3 Vocabulary

Making an effort

(a) Find the <u>underlined</u> expressions in the text in Exercise 1 which mean:

1 finding something very difficult ....

2 without enthusiasm or real interest ....

3 make a lot of effort to do something ....

4 (to get the right result) by experimenting ....

5 do something without having to make much effort ....

6 find all your effort very rewarding ....

7 do something the right way ....

8 making a mistake ....

(b) Complete the text with the expressions from Exercise 3a in the correct form.

Mum and Dad have always ¹................ to make sure I have a happy family life, and so I wanted to do something for them. So I decided to become an expert in washing up. And I mean an expert – this wasn't something I was going to do ²................ . I was going to be the best. At first I ³................ and I didn't always ⁴................ to get those knives and forks as clean as I wanted. Occasionally a plate would fall from my hands and break on the floor but I wasn't going to give up.

I found the best washing-up detergent through ⁵................ . I must have experimented with more than a dozen before I found one that ⁶................ the job ....

After weeks of practice I had finally become what I wanted to be – the best washer-up in the world. And I admit I used to ⁷................ looking at that rack of shining plates, glasses and dishes. I felt proud.

And then one day I came home from school, all excited at the thought of washing up after the evening meal, and there it was standing right in the middle of the kitchen – all sparkling and new. My parents had bought a dish washer. Had I ⁸................ ?

(c) Work with a partner. Use the expressions in Exercise 3b to talk about things you've learned to do.

I learned to play the guitar through trial and error.

At first I struggled with reading the music.

4 Pronunciation

Linking sounds (intrusive /w/ and /j/)

◁)) Turn to page 120.

5 Listen and speak

a Look at the photos. Complete the sentences, then match two of the sentences with each photo.

bring   did   left   takes   won   did

1   I _____ English literature at university because of this passion.
2   He _____ it up until it looked shiny and beautiful again.
3   He had _____ me his collection of books.
4   He _____ a scholarship to Cambridge to study music.
5   It _____ me back to a precise moment when my grandmother and I were together.
6   It would always _____ us good luck.

b 🔊 Listen to the three people talking about a special possession they inherited from a relative. Check your answers to Exercise 5a.

c 🔊 Listen again and choose answer a, b or c.

1   Why did Ceri originally develop such a passion for reading?
   a   Because her father taught her to read at an early age.
   b   Because she wanted to make her father proud.
   c   Because she loved stories.

2   How did the rest of her family react to Ceri and her father's love of books?
   a   They ignored it.
   b   They were a bit jealous and probably wanted to join in.
   c   It made her mother and brother really angry.

3   Why did Guy's grandfather never become a professional musician?
   a   Because he wanted a job that paid more money.
   b   Because he wasn't good enough.
   c   Because his father didn't approve.

4   What are the strongest memories that Guy has of the piano?
   a   His grandfather playing beautiful music on it.
   b   His grandfather teaching him how to play it.
   c   The day his grandfather sold it.

5   Why was Paula surprised to see the stone in the box?
   a   Because she didn't know her grandmother had kept it.
   b   Because it wasn't as valuable as the other objects.
   c   Because she had forgotten all about it.

6   Why is the stone so important to Paula now?
   a   Because it reminds her of her childhood and the time she spent with her grandmother.
   b   Because she thought it had been lost for ever.
   c   Because it brings good luck.

Ceri Chamberlain

Paula Cocozza

Guy Jowett

d Think about the best present you ever received. Make notes under the headings.

1 What was it?
2 Who gave it to you?
3 Why was it so special?

e Work in small groups. Talk about the best present you ever received.

6 Grammar

Modal verbs review

a Look at the examples from the listening text. Can you remember which present the words in italics refer to? Write B for book, P for piano and S for stone.

1 She must have kept *it* in her purse and carried it with her. ....*S*....
2 How could anybody play *it* so beautifully? ....
3 I may even get lessons on *it* again. ....
4 My grandmother told me we should look for *one*. ....
5 You couldn't start reading *it* before the other person was there. ....
6 Maybe one day I'll write someone else a note and leave *it* to them. ....
7 I asked him if I could buy *it* from him. ....

b Circle the modal verb in each sentence.

c Match the sentences in Exercise 6a to these uses of the modal verb. Write the number of the sentence next to each use.

a make a prediction ....7....
b ask for permission (in the past) ....
c talk about a possible future event ....
d express a prohibition (something that is not allowed) in the past ....
e talk about ability in the past ....
f express an obligation ....
g make a deduction about something in the past ....
h make a suggestion ....

d Circle the correct options.

1 What do you think we *may / should* get Mum for her birthday?
2 Promise me you *won't / can't* sing 'Happy Birthday'.
3 She's going to be thirty next week. She *must / can't* be very happy because she doesn't like getting older.
4 She *can / may* say 'happy birthday' in twenty different languages.
5 *May / Would* I ask you how old you are?
6 I *might / can* go to her party. I'm not sure yet.
7 I *would / will* be very angry if my father forgot my birthday.
8 You *can / must* remember to write your grandmother a 'thank you' letter.

7 Speak

a Complete the questions with a modal verb. Compare answers with a partner.

1 What presents .... you most like to get for your next birthday?
2 If you have a birthday party, what things .... you do to make sure it's a success?
3 Imagine it was your best friend's birthday and you couldn't afford a present. What things .... you give him/her?
4 How do you think you .... feel when it's your 40th birthday?

b Now discuss the questions with a different partner.

Culture in mind

8 Read

a Read the text and write the names of the countries under the pictures.

Birthday traditions in different countries

Birthdays are celebrated all over the world. Some traditions are fairly similar from country to country: candles, cakes and birthday wishes, birthday games and pinches for good luck.

Other customs are quite different. Here are a few.

Argentina – In Argentina, as in many Latin American countries, one of the most important birthday parties is a girl's fifteenth. When girls turn 15 they have a huge party and dance the waltz first with their father, and then the boys at the party.

China – First the birthday child pays respect to the parents and receives a gift of money. Friends and relatives are invited to lunch, and noodles are served to wish the birthday child a long life.

Denmark – A flag is flown outside a window to show that someone who lives in that house is having a birthday. Presents are placed around the child's bed while they are sleeping so they will see them immediately when they wake up.

The Netherlands – Special year birthdays such as 5, 10, 15, 20, 21 are called 'crown' years and the birthday child receives an especially large gift. The family also decorates the birthday child's chair with flowers or paper streamers, paper flowers and balloons.

India – Usually Indian children wear white to school. However, on their birthday children wear coloured clothes to school and give out chocolates to everyone in the class. Their best friend helps them to do this.

Israel – A small child sits in a chair while adults lift it up and down a number of times corresponding to the child's age, plus one for good luck.

Japan – The birthday child wears new clothes to mark the occasion. Certain birthdays are more important than others and these are celebrated with a visit to the local shrine. These are the third and seventh birthdays for girls and the fifth for boys.

(b) Read the texts again. Write the names of the country or countries.

In which country (or countries):

1 is money traditionally given?
2 does everyone celebrate their birthday on the same day?
3 are sweets involved?
4 is the birthday made known to the outside world?
5 are there some birthdays that are more important than others?
6 does dancing play an important part?
7 are special clothes worn?
8 is a chair involved?

Discussion box

Work in pairs or small groups. Discuss these questions together.

1 What do you do on your birthday?
2 What birthday traditions are there in your country?
3 Do you think these traditions are dying out? If so, why?
4 Do you have any personal/family traditions? Tell the class about them.

(e)

Mexico – The piñata is a big hollow animal usually made out of papier mâché. It is filled with goodies and hung from the ceiling. The birthday child is blindfolded and hits the piñata until it breaks open and then all the children share the sweets.

Vietnam – Everyone celebrates their birthdays on New Year's Day, or Tet as it is known in Vietnam. The Vietnamese do not acknowledge the exact day they were born. A baby is considered to be one year old on Tet no matter when they were born that year. On the first morning of Tet, adults congratulate children on becoming a year older by presenting them with red envelopes that contain 'Lucky Money,' or *li xi*.

9 Write

(a) Read the summary of the text in Exercise 1. Is it a good summary or not?

> It all started when Danny Wallace, 26, from London was bored. He put an ad on the internet and asked people to join him. Now, he is the head of 'Join Me' – a club whose members do good deeds for strangers every Friday.
>
> Many Londoners don't talk to each other. This is why Danny Wallace usually goes out on Fridays. He sometimes goes to cafés and sometimes talks to strangers, and then he usually walks away. Sometimes people are surprised, and sometimes they are suspicious. Danny Wallace says that it is important to smile and look confident. Then people are not suspicious when they see you. And he also says that one should not be nervous, because if you are nervous, people sometimes hit you and run away, and that's not very kind.
>
> Join Me is without geographical boundaries, but there are quite a few members in London and I get quite a lot of stories about things they have done on the Tube or on the buses. One lady got on the bus and put a £10 note down and said: 'That's for me and the next nine people' so at every stop, everyone who got on was told it was paid for. There are lots of stories about what Londoners have done on buses and in the Underground. Danny thinks that when you live in London, you should not put your head down, and you should also not become angry at other people. He is also of the opinion that people should apologise if they step on someone else's foot.

(b) Read the summary again and check the following:

1 Does it include the key points from each paragraph of the text in Exercise 1?
2 Has the writer of the summary copied whole sentences from the original text?

(c) Re-write the summary in Exercise 9a. Improve the summary, using the guide below to help you.

- When writing a summary, read the text and make notes about the main ideas.
- Read the text again. Underline the key points in each paragraph.
- Write the summary. Make sure you cover all the key points.
- It is OK to use good phrases from the original text *verbatim* (word for word), but don't copy longer pieces of text. And remember that, if you do use original text, it should be in quotation marks.

Peacemakers

* Past perfect passive
* Past perfect continuous
* Vocabulary: conflicts and solutions

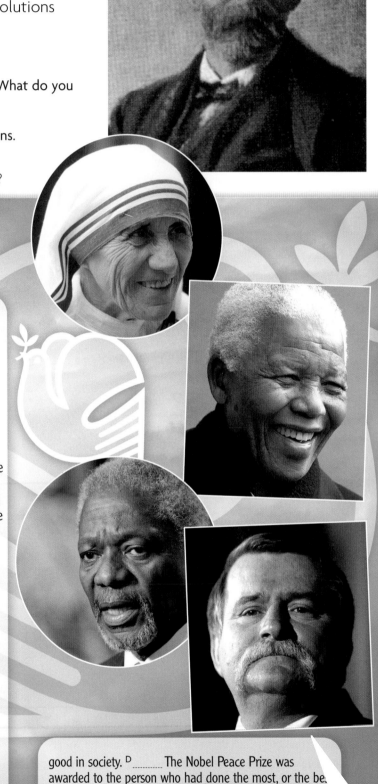

1 Read

(a) Do you recognise the people in the photos? What do you know about them?

(b) Read the text quickly and answer the questions.

1 How did Alfred Nobel make his money?

2 Why did he decide to start the Nobel Prizes?

Alfred Nobel
Rests in Peace

People like Martin Luther King Jr, Nelson Mandela, Aung San Suu Kyi, Kofi Annan, Lech Walesa and Mother Teresa have become famous all around the world. A _____ They are all winners of the Nobel Peace Prize. But none of them would have received their prize and the recognition it brings if it had not been for one Swedish man, Alfred Nobel.

When Alfred joined the Nobel family company, it had been developing explosives for many years. Alfred's father, Immanuel, had started the family fortune by working for the Russian army to produce landmines and seamines, which are bombs that are put under the ground or in the sea, and explode when people move over them. But the family made even more money by manufacturing nitro-glycerine, which was an effective but very dangerous explosive.
One day Alfred arrived home to find that his 20-year-old brother Emil had been killed in a nitro-glycerine explosion.
B _____ The result was dynamite, which became an immediate success all over the world.

Alfred Nobel always wanted dynamite to be used for peaceful means. And when it was used to blast a path for the Panama Canal in 1914 he couldn't have been happier. Unfortunately, in the same year, the First World War started, and, when it ended four years later, dynamite had been used to take away the lives of thousands of young men. C _____ To see his invention being used in this way made him very sad.

Sometime later Alfred's older brother Ludwig died. One newspaper accidentally printed Alfred's obituary instead of his brother's. The obituary described Alfred as a man who had become rich by inventing a weapon of mass destruction. When Alfred read this review of his life, he was very unhappy and decided to do something about it. He decided that he would use the great fortune that he had made to reward people who had been working to promote good in society. D _____ The Nobel Peace Prize was awarded to the person who had done the most, or the be[st] work to promote friendship between countries, to abolish armies and to hold and promote peace conferences.

In 1997 the Nobel Peace Prize went to an American called Jody Williams for her efforts to get landmines banned. E _____ Perhaps now, Alfred Nobel will rest more easily in his grave.

c 🔊 Read the text again and add the sentences. Listen and check.

1 Alfred became determined to invent a safer explosive.
2 The five awards he created were for physics, chemistry, medicine, literature and, most significantly, peace.
3 Ironically, of course, the Nobel family fortunes had been built on mines.
4 Alfred had always hated war and considered it to be 'the horror of horrors and the greatest of all crimes'.
5 And what do they have in common?

d Read the text again and put these events in order.

1 Alfred started working with his father. ☐
2 Alfred read about his own 'death' in a newspaper. ☐
3 Alfred's brother Emil died in an accident. ☐
4 Dynamite killed many people during the First World War. ☐
5 Alfred created the Nobel Prizes. ☐
6 Alfred invented dynamite. ☐
7 The Nobel company made mines. ☐
8 Dynamite was used to build the Panama Canal. ☐

2 Grammar

Past perfect passive

a Complete these sentences from the text in Exercise 1.

1 One day he arrived home to find that his brother .... killed in an explosion.
2 When the war ended four years later, dynamite .... used to take away the lives of thousands of young men.

b Circle the correct options to complete the rule.

> **Rule:**
> • We form the past perfect passive with the past perfect form of the verb *be / have* plus the *infinitive / past participle* of the main verb.

c Read the text about the end of the First World War and circle the correct verb forms.

At 11 o'clock on the 11th November, 1918, the peace treaty that ended the First World War ¹*was signed / had been signed* in a railway carriage. When the war ended, the soldiers of all the armies ²*were sent / had been sent* home, but millions of men ³*were killed / had been killed* in the fighting and vast amounts of money ⁴*were spent / had been spent*. Large parts of the French countryside were in terrible condition, and many towns and cities ⁵*were destroyed / had been destroyed* by the guns of the opposing armies.

Because of the destruction, a decision ⁶*was taken / had been taken* in 1919 to start the League of Nations, to make sure that such a war would never happen again. The idea of a League ⁷*was discussed / had been discussed* for several years before 1919, but it was the First World War that made it happen.

Unfortunately, the League of Nations didn't work. Between 1939 and 1945, another World War ⁸*was fought / had been fought* between countries all over the world.

d Complete the sentences. Use the past simple passive or past perfect passive form of the verbs in brackets.

1 When the soldiers got home, they discovered that their homes .... (destroy).
2 When we got to the bookshop, we were too late! The last copy .... (sell).
3 There was a terrible car accident in my street last night – one man .... (kill).
4 The 2006 football World Cup .... (hold) in Germany.
5 I was angry when I got to the shop because my bicycle .... (not repair) yet.
6 It was strange to see my old school again – all the walls .... (paint) a different colour.

3 Listen

(a) 🔊 Listen to an interview with foreign correspondent, Martin Davies. Answer the questions.

1 Where is Martin Davies?
2 What are they celebrating in Nairobi?
3 What issue is often a source of conflict, according to Martin Davies?
4 Why are men in Africa proud?
5 What does Martin Davies say will be one of the most important issues in Africa in the next few years?

(b) 🔊 Listen to the interview again. Martin Davies makes the following points in the interview. Put them in the order in which you hear them.

☐ The prize will help to overcome prejudices against women.

☐ Martin Davies praises people who take risks for what they believe in.

☐ Professor Maathai's work will encourage people who work for the environment.

☐ He mentions examples of people who *fought for what they believed in*.

☐ Wangari Maathai feels overwhelmed that her work has been recognised by the Nobel Committee.

Discussion box

Work in pairs or small groups. Discuss these questions together.

1 Martin Luther King, Nelson Mandela and Bishop Tutu are mentioned in the interview. What do you know about their work?

2 If you could award a Nobel Peace Prize, who would you give it to? Why?

4 Grammar

Past perfect continuous

(a) Read the example then circle the correct option to complete the rule.

When they received their prizes they had been working for many years for the things they believed in.

Rule:
● We use the past perfect continuous to talk about *continuous / single* actions that began *before / at the same time as* a specific time in the past.

(b) Underline another example of the past perfect continuous in the text in Exercise 1a.

(c) Circle the correct verb forms.

Last Friday evening, Arlene was on a train to London. She ¹*was going / had been going* home. She was hungry because she ²*didn't eat / hadn't eaten* for several hours, and she was tired because she ³*had travelled / had been travelling* for almost a day. Yet she was happy, too, because she ⁴*had received / had been receiving* a letter from her parents. She was also happy because she ⁵*had looked / had been looking* forward to going home ever since the day she left.

(d) Complete the sentences with the past continuous or past perfect continuous form of the verbs in brackets.

1 When my alarm clock went off, I .... (sleep) for eleven hours.

2 Her face was red and she had a handkerchief in her hand, so I knew she .... (cry).

3 I met an old friend of mine yesterday when I .... (shop).

4 When she finally got to see the doctor, she .... (wait) for over an hour.

5 A car almost hit me when I .... (cross) the road last Saturday.

6 I .... (think) about the problem for hours, when suddenly the answer came into my head!

5 Vocabulary

Conflicts and solutions

(a) Complete the sentences from the interview with *find / resolve*.

1 Natural resources are a source of conflict, and often there are peaceful ways to .... the conflict.

2 They had been trying to .... solutions to the problems around them.

(b) Read this webpage. Match the underlined expressions with definitions a–h. Write 1–8 next to the definitions.

Friendsagain.com
– we are here to help you!

If you have a disagreement with a neighbour, a friend or a partner, and can't seem to resolve it, don't worry, we're here to help. Sometimes people ¹fall out completely, and even when they try to ²sort things out between each other, they ³get stuck and are unable to ⁴make up. Problems like this can easily be sorted out if you know the best way to do it.

And we know the best way! We have years of experience in managing and ⁵resolving conflicts. We believe that it is always possible to ⁶reach a compromise that satisfies everyone involved. We do everything we can to ⁷stay neutral. We're not interested in ⁸taking sides, we're only interested in helping you to end the deadlock.

So contact us and let us help you find a solution.

a not support one person more than another ....

b have a disagreement and no longer be friendly ....

c to be unable to go any further ....

d be friendly again after a disagreement ....

e find an answer that is acceptable to both people ....

f finding a way to end disagreements or fights ....

g to make things clearer/better ....

h support one person against another ....

(c) Complete the sentences with the underlined expressions in Exercise 5b. Then listen and check.

1 He's a bit upset because he's .... with his best friend.

2 Can you help me with my Maths homework? I keep ....

3 Let's .... I'll do the washing up if you cook me dinner. OK?

4 I get angry at home because my parents always .... my brother's ....

5 The presidents of the two countries are meeting to try and .... that started last month.

6 Annie can help you with any problems you've got. She's really good at .... them ....

7 Haven't you and your brother .... yet? I'm tired of seeing the two of you fighting all the time!

8 There are many countries in the world that always .... when a war starts.

6 Pronunciation

Linking sounds

Turn to page 120.

7 Speak

Read the text. Work in groups and discuss how the conflict described in the text could be resolved.

Monica is brilliant at maths. One of her best friends in class, Jake, has asked her several times to help him with his maths homework. She has always been happy to help him, but recently the situation has started to get uncomfortable because Jake has stopped doing the homework himself and has started copying it from her.

Yesterday Mr Donovan, their maths teacher, confronted Monica with the situation and accused her of letting Jake copy the homework from her. Monica confessed to it, but Jake was furious when he found out.

How could the situation be resolved?

8 Listen and speak

a 🔊 Look at the picture and the title of the song. What do you think the singer feels about *Peace, Love and Understanding*? Listen to the song (with your books closed) and check your ideas.

(What's so funny about) Peace, Love and Understanding?

by Elvis C...

As I walk through this wicked ¹place
Searching for light in the darkness of insanity,
I ask myself – is all hope lost?
Is there only ²anger and hatred and misery?

And each time I feel like this inside,
There's one thing I want to ³see:

What's so funny about peace love & understanding?
What's so funny about peace love & understanding?

And as I walk on through troubled ⁴days,
My spirit gets so downhearted sometimes.
So where are the strong, and who are the trusted?
And where is the harmony?
Sweet harmony.

'Cause each time I feel it slipping away, it just makes
   me want to ⁵shout.
What's so funny about peace love & understanding?
What's so funny about peace love & understanding?

So where are the strong?
And who are the trusted?
And where is the harmony?
Sweet harmony.

'Cause each time I feel it slipping away, it just makes
   me want to cry.
What's so funny about peace love & understanding?
(repeated)

Did you know ...?

This song, written by Englishman Nick Lowe, has been recorded by many people, including Lowe and Costello.

It was also performed by Bob Geldof at the Nelson Mandela AIDS Day concert in Cape Town, in 2003. Over 40,000 people attended a three-hour show, which was also seen by 2 billion people on TV. Peter Gabriel, Bono, Beyonce, Yusuf Islam (formerly Cat Stevens), Queen and Eurythmics were among the 23 artists who performed live.

b 🔊 Listen again. The six underlined words in the lyrics are wrong. Write the correct words.

c The singer asks: *What's so funny about peace love & understanding?* What does he mean when he says *funny*?

a It makes you laugh.
b It's strange.

Why do you think he asks this question?

9 Write

(a) Read the text about a Nobel Prize winner. Which paragraph describes:

   a the writer's own opinion of this person?

   b the person's biographical history?

   c the person's achievements?

   d who the person is?

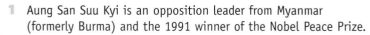

Aung San Suu Kyi

1 Aung San Suu Kyi is an opposition leader from Myanmar (formerly Burma) and the 1991 winner of the Nobel Peace Prize.

2 When she was two years old, her father, who was likely to become prime minister of independent Burma, was assassinated. She went to school in Burma until 1960, when her mother became ambassador to India. After studying in India, she attended the University of Oxford, where she met her future husband. She had two children and lived a rather quiet life until 1988, when she returned to Myanmar to look after her mother.

3 When Aung San Suu Kyi arrived in her country, people were protesting against the rule of the military government. On one occasion, hundreds of protesters were killed by the army, and this was the reason that Aung San Suu Kyi began to speak out. She began a non-violent struggle for democracy and human rights. She joined the National League for Democracy, which won more than 80 per cent of the parliamentary seats in 1990, but the military government ignored the results. Aung San Suu Kyi was placed under house arrest from July 1989. The military offered to free her if she agreed to leave Myanmar, but she refused to do so until the country was returned to civilian government and political prisoners were freed. She was freed from house arrest in July 1995.

4 I admire Aung San Suu Kyi for what she has done for the people of her country. Although she must have known from the very beginning that speaking out against the dictatorship in her country could be very dangerous for herself personally, she believed in her dream of a free Myanmar and continued her fight for democracy and human rights. I think as an opposition leader, Aung San Suu Kyi has set a perfect example of what politicians should be like. They should see themselves as serving the people of their country, rather than aiming to gain personal advantages, money and a life of luxury. Aung San Suu Kyi has very courageously shown the world what one woman, who never gave up her ideals, can achieve through peaceful means.

(b) Read the last paragraph of the text again. What things does the writer admire about Aung San Suu Kyi? How does the writer express his/her admiration?

(c) Write about a person you admire. Use the notes to help you. Write about 200–250 words.

   1 Decide on the person you want to write about. Make notes about what you already know about them. Use the internet or an encyclopaedia to find more information.

   2 Think about the structure of your text. Organise your information into paragraphs. Use the text in Exercise 9a to help you. Decide on which information the reader will find interesting. You don't have to include every detail.

   3 Consider why you have chosen this person. Ask yourself what the person has achieved, what is special about the person and what you admire about him/her.

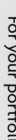

For your portfolio

Module 2 Check your progress

1 Grammar

a Rewrite the sentence or sentences using the sentence starter.

1 Mary's really pushy. I don't like this about her.

What I _don't like about Mary is that she's really pushy._

2 Playing with fire is dangerous.

It's _dangerous to play with fire._

3 He's always singing. This makes him seem friendly.

What makes ....

4 Keep calm. That's important.

It's ....

5 Paul always interrupts when I speak. I find this really annoying.

What I ....

6 Speaking a foreign language is fun.

It's ....

7 She told me she wanted something for her birthday. But I've forgotten now.

I've forgotten ....

8 We all forget people's names sometimes. That's normal.

It's ....

| | 6 |

b Complete the sentences. ~~Cross out~~ *would* when it is not possible to use it.

1 My mother *used to / would* be a nurse.

2 My father *used to / would* write me a letter every week.

3 They *used to / would* go for long walks on the beach every Sunday.

4 I *used to / would* live in London.

5 Our neighbours *used to / would* keep us awake with their loud music every weekend.

6 She *used to / would* be a really good ballet dancer when she was younger.

| | 6 |

c Circle the correct word in each sentence.

1 I don't think we *should / can / might* have told him.

2 What *can / will / would* you do if you were me?

3 Take a coat. I think it *must / can / may* get cold later.

4 *May / Must / Should* I ask you a personal question, please?

5 I'm sorry but I *wouldn't / can't / must* help you.

6 I really *may / can / must* remember to phone him tomorrow.

7 I *can / might / must* go away this weekend but I'm not sure yet.

| | 6 |

d Use the correct form of the verb to complete the sentences.

1 I remember .... (see) the car coming towards me but nothing after that.

2 Have you tried .... (phone) John at home? He might have left work early.

3 We stopped .... (have) a cup of coffee for ten minutes.

4 I tried .... (apologise) to him but he thought I was lying.

5 You must remember .... (invite) Carl to your party. He'll be upset if you forget.

6 I stopped .... (play) football after I broke my leg.

7 I don't remember .... (buy) this CD. Are you sure it's mine?

| | 7 |

e Use the verb in brackets in the past perfect simple or the past perfect passive to complete the sentences.

1 When we got to the party, all the food _had been eaten_ (eat) and there was nothing left for us.

2 By the time I got to the party she .... already .... (go) home.

3 I opened my wallet and found that I .... (left) all my money at home.

4 The police discovered the letter .... (write) two days before the murder.

5 When we got to the cinema we found that all the tickets .... (sell) so we went back home again.

6 After five minutes I realised I .... (see) the film before.

| | 5 |

f Circle the correct option.

1 I was tired because I *had worked / had been working* all day.

2 He didn't have any money because he *had spent / had been spending* it all on a new computer.

3 She *had waited / had been waiting* for three hours outside the café, and she wasn't very happy.

4 They *had eaten / had been eating* too much and they didn't feel very well.

5 I *had sat down / had been sitting down* all afternoon so I decided to go for a walk.

| | 5 |

2 Vocabulary

a (Circle) the correct word to complete each sentence.

1 He's always *by / in / on* a hurry. He needs to slow down a bit.

2 You said that *by / in / on* purpose. Why are you so mean to me?

3 When we heard the explosion, everyone started running *by / in / on* a panic.

4 I'm telling you this *by / in / on* secret. I don't want you to tell anyone.

5 We met *by / in / on* accident. We were both on the same train.

6 Could you leave me alone, please? I want to do this *by / in / on* private.

6

b Complete each sentence using a word from the box.

> properly   heartedly   error   find   struggled
> wrong   lengths

1 I don't mind changing school. I _____ it really easy to make new friends.

2 This is not right. I think I've done something _____ .

3 The only way to get the perfect haircut is through trial and _____ .

4 You shouldn't have said that. She went to great _____ to try and please you.

5 When we moved to Paris, I _____ a lot with French for a year or so but now I speak it quite well.

6 She did it really half-_____ . I don't think she really wanted to do it.

7 I tried to do it _____ but I made too many mistakes.

7

c Match the sentence halves.

1 Dave and his brother have fallen

2 Have you and your mum made

3 You should talk to Sue and try to sort

4 I'm sure if you talk, you can reach

5 I know you're unhappy but I'm not taking

6 I'm finding it difficult to stay

a out all your problems.

b sides with either of you on this issue.

c neutral – Jean's my best friend.

d a compromise so you're both happy.

e up yet? Or are you still angry with her?

f out about something.

6

d Read the descriptions and complete the puzzle. Use personality adjectives.

Across

1 Bob always understands how I feel and he's always ready to listen to my problems.

3 Sue's really funny. She makes me laugh a lot.

4 Henry doesn't always pay attention to what he does and this means that he makes mistakes.

5 Jenny's always so pleased with everything that she does. It annoys me a bit.

6 You can never feel miserable when Pete's around.

Down

2 Dave prefers a game of chess to a game of football.

4 Kevin always says exactly what I want to hear. He makes me feel good about myself.

5 You can't have a serious conversation about anything with Jane.

8

How did you do?

Tick (✓) a box for each section.

Total score:	Very good	😐 OK	🙁 Not very good
62			
Grammar	27 – 35	18 – 26	less than 18
Vocabulary	21 – 27	14 – 20	less than 14

YOU WILL LEARN ABOUT ...

- An unusual event to raise money for charity ....
- Threats to our environment ....
- Ways of reducing the amount of energy we use ....
- How famous people are helping the United Nations ....
- Two concerts that tried to make a difference to our world ....
- Fair Trade ....

✱ Can you match each picture with a topic?

YOU WILL LEARN HOW TO ...

Speak
- Discuss the ages that children should be allowed to do certain things
- Talk about ways you can get involved
- Discuss the global issues that worry you the most
- Talk about ways you can cut down on the amount of energy you use
- Talk about famous people in your country
- Give your opinion on issues such as smoking in public places, graffiti and whale hunting
- Discuss ways of making the world a fairer place
- Talk about foreign products that you buy and use in your country

Write
- A formal letter to raise money for charity
- A magazine article about life in the future
- A discursive essay on pop stars and politics
- A report on a class survey

Read
- A weblog about a trip to Mount Everest
- An extract from *Lord of the Flies*
- A newspaper article about the dangers our Earth faces
- An article on UN Goodwill Ambassadors
- An account of Live Aid and Live8
- An article about Fair Trade

Listen
- A radio phone-in programme about giving the vote to 16 year-olds
- A radio programme about alternative energy supplies
- People giving their opinion about famous people in politics
- A web announcement about the make-up of our world
- A song called *One World (not three)*

Use grammar

Can you match the names of the grammar points with the examples?

Mixed conditionals	You have **until** tomorrow to give me your answer.
Future perfect	He'll love it, **won't he**?
Future continuous	If you **had brought** the map, we **wouldn't be** lost now.
Future time markers	Half the world **gets by** on less than $1 a day.
Reduced relative clauses	I'**ll be sunbathing** on a beach this time next week.
Question tags	If she **had told** you, you **would have been** angry.
Phrasal verbs	*Imagine* is **the song most played** on British radio.
Revision of conditionals	He'**ll have** forgotten by tomorrow.

Use vocabulary

Can you think of two more examples for each topic?

Ways of saving energy	Global issues	Expressing opinions	Imprecise numbers
switch off lights	global warming	to my mind	about
recycle paper	pollution	if you ask me	roughly
....	....	....	....
....	....	....	....

Get involved

* Conditional review
* Mixed conditionals
* Vocabulary: ways of getting involved

Show Racism the Red Card

1 Read and listen

(a) Look at the photos and discuss the questions with a partner. Where are these people? What are they doing? Why do you think they are doing this?

http://www.walkingbackblog.co.uk/day10.html

WALKING BACK Everest Blog

Day 1 — Am I mad?
I first heard of 'Show Racism the Red Card' when a friend asked me to sign a petition supporting their work. Basically, it's an organisation which uses professional footballers to help fight racism in sport and society. I liked the idea, so I signed.

A few weeks later, he asked me if I wanted to do a bit more for them. I thought he probably meant make a donation or do some voluntary work. But then he told me that a group of about 20 people were getting sponsored to play the highest ever game of rugby at 5,140 metres on the slopes of Mount Everest. Well, to cut a long story short, tomorrow I'm off to Nepal. Wish me luck.

Day 4 — Uphill all the way
We're making our way up to the base camp — that's where most climbers start their final ascent to the top — and then, we'll play our game. There's one thing I've learned pretty quickly. If you walk too fast at high altitude, you get really short of breath. There's not much oxygen, and you have to do everything slowly. Today we started out at 8am. We had to cross three suspension bridges. One of them was so high you couldn't see the bottom. Then we walked through some beautiful forest areas before we started a two-hour uphill hike to Namche Bazaar. It was really tough and most of us had headaches when we arrived. Tomorrow we're going to have a rest day. I need one!

Day 5 — A welcome rest
Today I'm wondering why I always do things the hard way. I mean most people go on demonstrations or hand out leaflets in the High Street if they want to help out, but me — no. I have to go up Mount Everest and play a game of rugby. Anyway, today was a day off so I went into town and bought a monkey hat and a blanket for my sleeping bag. We're surrounded by mountains here — it's beautiful. I took lots of photos. If I have time later, I'll upload some of them onto the blog, so you can all see where I am.

Day 10 — On top of the world
Base camp is basically just a lot of stones and tents. The walk up was really exhausting. Maybe if I was fitter, I wouldn't find this so hard, but then it's not just me — all of us get very short of breath. We passed two crashed helicopters just to show you how dangerous Everest can be. One of them crashed only two days ago. No one was killed, luckily.

Day 11 — The game
Today we played our game. It was supposed to be a 'friendly', and last night, we had agreed we'd just walk and not run. However, it got competitive and two players were even sent off. We only played for 14 minutes. I think someone would have got hurt if we'd played any longer! My team won and I scored the last try! Of course, none of this matters. What's really important is that we did it and we've raised a load of money. It feels amazing.

(b) Read Mike's weblog quickly to check your answers.

(c) 🔊 Read the text again and listen. On what day did the following things happen?

1 The group had a rest from their climb.
2 Mike travelled to Nepal.
3 Many of them didn't feel well after a difficult walk up to a local town.
4 The group decided they would take the game easy.
5 Mike went shopping.
6 A helicopter crashed.

Discussion box

Work in pairs or small groups. Discuss these questions together.

1 Have you ever helped raise money for charity? In what way?
2 Do you think it's a good idea to raise money in this way? Why / Why not?
3 What unusual ideas for raising money have you heard or read about?

2 Grammar

Conditionals review

(a) Look at the examples from the text and complete the table.

A *Someone would have got hurt if we'd played any longer.*

B *If I have time later, I'll upload some of the photos onto the blog.*

C *If you walk too fast at high altitude, you get really short of breath.*

D *Maybe if I was fitter, I wouldn't find this so hard.*

	Example sentence	If clause	Main clause
Zero conditional		present simple	
First conditional	B		
Second conditional			would(n't) + infinitive
Third conditional			past perfect

(b) Which of these conditional types is used to talk about:

1 A hypothetical situation and consequence in the past which is, therefore, impossible to change?
2 A condition and consequence that are always true?
3 A hypothetical situation in the present and its future consequence which may be very unlikely or impossible to happen?
4 A possible present situation and its possible future consequence?

(c) Look at some more entries from Mike's weblog and decide which type of conditional they are.

1 If it wasn't so cold at night, I wouldn't sleep so badly.
2 There are easier things to do if you want to raise money for charity.
3 Do you get a really bad headache if you walk too fast?
4 I wouldn't have made so many new friends if I hadn't agreed to come on this trip.
5 I won't be able to play the game tomorrow if I'm feeling this ill.
6 If we stop in Namche Bazaar on the way down, I'll buy some more things.
7 Would I have made it to the base camp if we hadn't had that rest day?

3 Vocabulary

Ways of getting involved

(a) Complete the leaflet with the words in the box. Look back at the text in Exercise 1a to help you.

> hand out do get sign make
> go on

Support us and get involved.

Six things that <u>you</u> can do!

1 Visit our internet site and _____ our petition.
2 _____ our demonstration in the park this Sunday.
3 _____ leaflets in the street.
4 _____ a donation.
5 Do something unusual and _____ sponsored *to raise* money for us.
6 _____ some voluntary *work* for us – we always need people to help out in the office!

(b) Work in pairs. Discuss the questions. Use the vocabulary from Exercise 3a.

1 Have you ever signed a petition / been on a demonstration / been sponsored to do something?
2 Have you done any voluntary work?

4 Listen

a What is the connection between the words in the box?

> to vote   an election   the government   to run a country

b 🔊 Listen to a radio talk show and tick the correct boxes.

	older than 16	16 or younger
Trevor	☐	☐
Jenny	☐	☐
Laurence	☐	☐

c 🔊 Listen again and choose a, b or c.

1 Trevor thinks
   a politicians are corrupt.
   b young people are too immature.
   c politics needs new ideas.

2 Jenny thinks
   a you should pass a test if you want to vote.
   b we should give young people the chance to vote.
   c young people don't trust politicians.

3 Laurence thinks
   a that people who pay taxes should be able to vote.
   b young people are more interested in personal power.
   c politics has changed.

d 🔊 Listen again. Who ...

1 didn't talk about current issues when they were at school?
2 says young people really care about current issues?
3 thinks that an exam to find out which young people could vote is a bad idea?
4 really believes that young people could vote sensibly?
5 is a teacher?
6 suggests that young people could be given the vote if they pay taxes?
7 thinks that politicians could take advantage of young voters?

Discussion box

Work in pairs or small groups. Discuss these questions together.

1 What questions do you think the test should include?
2 Which of the callers do you agree with?
3 Which of the callers do you disagree with?

5 Pronunciation

Contractions in third conditionals

🔊 Turn to page 121.

6 Grammar

Mixed conditionals

a Conditional sentences do not always follow the patterns you looked at in Exercise 2a. Look at these examples and answer the questions.

If young people <u>had the vote</u>, this government <u>wouldn't have won</u> the last election.

1   Do young people have the vote now?
2   Did the government win the last election?

If I <u>had learned</u> about politics at school, I think I <u>would understand</u> how to vote better today.

3   Did I learn about politics in school?
4   Do I understand how to vote better today?

b Complete the rules. Write *second* or *third*.

> **Rule:**
> ● When we want to talk about the past consequence of a situation that is still true at the time of speaking, we use a .... conditional in the *if* clause and a .... conditional in the main clause.
> ● When we want to talk about the present consequence of a past action, we use a .... conditional in the *if* clause and a .... conditional in the main clause.

c Match the two parts of the sentences.

1 If I hadn't gone to bed so late last night,	a I'd be feeling very tired now.
2 If I'd gone to bed late last night,	b I wouldn't have gone to see 'Nightfright' with you.
3 If I liked horror films,	c they'd be world champions now.
4 If I didn't like horror films,	d they wouldn't be world champions now.
5 If they hadn't lost that game,	e I wouldn't be feeling so tired today.
6 If they'd lost that game,	f I would've gone to see 'Nightfright' with you.

d Combine the two sentences to make mixed conditionals. Use the verb form in brackets to help you.

1   I ate too much last night. I'm feeling ill today. **(eaten)**

   If I hadn't eaten too much last night, I wouldn't be feeling ill today.

2   I really don't understand maths. I failed the test. **(understood)**
3   I spent all my money on CDs. I haven't got any money today. **(spent)**
4   I don't speak Spanish. I didn't understand what they said. **(spoke)**
5   I can't swim. I couldn't save the young girl. **(been able)**

7 Speak

a Work with a partner. Discuss the following:

At what ages do you think young people in the UK can do these things?

● buy a pet
● work part-time
● be legally responsible for a crime they commit
● drive
● buy a lottery ticket
● have a tattoo
● become a member of parliament
● leave school
● give blood
● borrow money from a bank

b Work with a partner. What are the age limits for these things in your country?

c Think of the consequences if the age limits were lower/higher.

If all kids had to stay at school until they were 18, the teachers would have a lot of trouble.

If I'd won the lottery when I was a child, I'd have spent all the money on sweets and toys.

d Discuss your ideas in small groups.

If I hadn't eaten too much last night, I wouldn't be feeling ill today.

Literature in mind

8 Read

(a) Look at the cover of the book and read the short summary of the story. Would you be interested in reading the book? Why (not)?

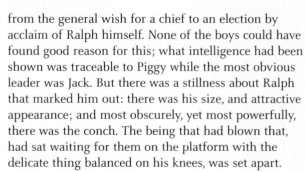

L⊕RD ⊕F THE FLIES
by William Golding

A plane carrying English schoolboys, including a choir, crashes and leaves all the boys as survivors on a desert island. How will they manage without adults? Ralph and his fat friend Piggy, Jack Merridew and the other boys, struggle for survival and then for domination.

(b) Read the text quickly. Who are the two candidates in the election and who wins?

Merridew turned to Ralph.
'Aren't there any grown-ups?'
'No.'
Merridew sat down on a trunk and looked around the circle.
'Then we'll have to look after ourselves.'
Secure on the other side of Ralph, Piggy spoke timidly.
'That's why Ralph made a meeting. So as we can decide what to do.' [...]

Jack spoke.
'We've got to decide about being rescued.'
There was a buzz. One of the small boys, Henry, said that he wanted to go home.
'Shut up,' said Ralph absently. He lifted the conch. 'Seems to me we ought to have a chief to decide things.'
'A chief! A chief!'
'I ought to be chief,' said Jack with simple arrogance, 'because I'm chapter chorister and head boy. I can sing C sharp.'
Another buzz.
'Well then,' said Jack, 'I ...'
He hesitated. The dark boy, Roger, stirred at last and spoke up.
'Let's have a vote.'
'Yes!'
'Vote for a chief!'
'Let's vote...!'
This toy of voting was almost as pleasing as the conch. Jack started to protest but the clamour changed from the general wish for a chief to an election by acclaim of Ralph himself. None of the boys could have found good reason for this; what intelligence had been shown was traceable to Piggy while the most obvious leader was Jack. But there was a stillness about Ralph that marked him out: there was his size, and attractive appearance; and most obscurely, yet most powerfully, there was the conch. The being that had blown that, had sat waiting for them on the platform with the delicate thing balanced on his knees, was set apart.
'Him with the shell.'
'Ralph! Ralph!'
'Let him be the chief with the trumpet-thing.'
Ralph raised his hand for silence.
'All right. Who wants Jack for chief?'
With dreary obedience the choir raised their hands.
'Who wants me?'
Every hand outside the choir except Piggy's was raised immediately. Then Piggy, too, raised his hand grudgingly into the air.
Ralph counted.
'I'm chief, then.'
The circle of boys broke into applause. Even the choir applauded; and the freckles on Jack's face disappeared under a blush of mortification. He started up, then changed his mind and sat down again while the air rang. Ralph looked at him, eager to offer something.
'The choir belongs to you, of course.'

c Read the text again and answer the questions.

1 What is the conch?
2 Why does Jack think he should be leader?
3 What makes Ralph an attractive choice for leader?
4 Who voted for Jack?
5 Who voted for Ralph?
6 Why do you think Ralph lets Jack be in charge of the choir?

Discussion box

Work in pairs or small groups. Discuss these questions together.

1 In what ways are the children trying to act like grown-ups?
2 In what ways do they show that they are children?
3 What do you think would happen if children this age were left without adult supervision for a long time?

9 Write

a Read the letter and answer the questions.

1 Who's the letter from?
2 What do they want to raise money for?
3 What are they organising?
4 What two kinds of sponsorship do they hope to get?
5 Is the letter to some friends or to a business?

b Read the letter again and answer the questions.

1 Where does the sender put his own address and the date?
2 How does James MacDonald start the letter?
3 Does James use any contracted verb forms (e.g. it's or I'm)?
4 How does James end the letter?

c Work in groups. Imagine you want to raise money for charity. Decide on a charity, what you're going to do and how you hope to raise money.

d Write a letter (max. 250 words) to a company and ask for their support. Include:

- what it is that you plan to do
- what you would like from them
- what you could offer them in return

Trent High School
16 York Street
ECCLES ES12 5JP

2nd May 2007

Dear Sir/Madam,

As I am sure you already know, next month will see the beginning of the *Have a Heart* campaign to raise money for heart research. As part of popular support for this campaign, several of the students here at Trent High School have decided to organise a half-marathon on the 28th June. Of course, all the money that we hope to raise by doing this will go to *Have a Heart*.

In order to raise as much money as possible, we are doing two things: a) asking members of the public to sponsor individual runners in the race, and b) looking for institutional sponsors to help with the fund-raising. It is for this second reason that I am writing to you now.

As the representative of Trent High School's half-marathon committee, I am writing to ask if your company would be willing to consider providing sponsorship for our event. What we had in mind, if you are agreeable, is to put the sponsor's name on the numbers of each runner, and to have the sponsor's name on banners along the route as well as at the finish line. We hope and believe that our sponsor will, in this way, gain a lot of positive publicity.

It is difficult, of course, to make a request for a specific amount of money, but we are hoping that the company which sponsors us would do so to the amount of £1,000.00 or more, and would perhaps also contribute to the making of banners etc.

Should you be interested, please contact us at the above address.

Thank you for giving our request your attention. We look forward to hearing from you.

Yours faithfully,

James MacDonald

10 SOS Earth

* Future continuous
* Future perfect
* Future time expressions
* Vocabulary: global issues
* Vocabulary: conserving energy

1 Read and listen

(a) Make a list of all the problems that you can think of facing our planet. Read through the newspaper article quickly to see how many of your ideas it mentions.

Time's Running Out

"Our planet is running out of time. Modern man has abused it so much that by 2050 we will have used up all of its resources. The Earth's population will need to find and colonise two planets as our forests and fresh water supplies vanish." (WWF)

This is the conclusion of a frightening report from the World Wide Fund for Nature (WWF) which experts will be discussing later this week in Geneva.

But will we really all be living in outer space fifty years from now? The answer is no. This is clearly unrealistic. The WWF are using this dramatic image in the hope that it will draw attention to the fact that now, more than ever, we need to take seriously the subject of how we treat our planet.

The report, based on scientific data from across the world, reveals that more than one third of the natural world has been destroyed by humans over the past three decades. Some of the frightening statistics it presents include:

● Since 1970 the cod population of the world's oceans has fallen from 264,000 tonnes to less than 60,000 tonnes. At this rate, the fish will have died out completely by 2030.

● Between 1970 and 2002 the planet's already heavily diminished forests were reduced by a further 12 per cent. In places such as South East Brazil, less than 7 per cent of the original forest remains.

● Black rhinoceros numbers have fallen from 65,000 in 1970 to around 3,100 now. The numbers of African elephants have fallen from around 1.2 million in 1980 to just over half a million while the population of tigers has fallen by 95 per cent during the past century.

As a way of measuring how much each country is responsible for the destruction of the planet, the report uses a system which it refers to as 'ecological footprints'. Each country's 'footprint' is calculated by looking at how much it consumes of the Earth's resources and how much it pollutes the atmosphere in a year. From these figures experts can calculate how much land is needed to support one inhabitant of each country. The more land that is needed, the higher the 'footprint'. Unsurprisingly, the report is particularly hard on the developed countries of North America, Europe and Asia. At the top of the list is America with a footprint of 12.2 hectares (that's about 18 football pitches), almost twice the average for Western European countries which is 6.28 hectares. At the bottom of the list are the African countries. In Ethiopia, for example, the 'footprint' is 2 hectares and in Burundi, the country that consumes least resources, it is just half a hectare.

The message is simple and clear. Unless people in the developed world start living in a more environmentally friendly way, fifty years from now there simply won't be enough resources to go round.

(b) 🔊 Read the text again and listen. Mark the statements *T* (true) or *F* (false). Correct the false ones.

1 The WWF think we will all be living on two new planets fifty years from now.

2 The report was written by scientists.

3 In the last thirty years we have used nearly 30 per cent of the Earth's natural resources.

4 Cod numbers have fallen by about 50 per cent since 1970.

5 There is none of the original forest left in South East Brazil.

6 The report blames countries like Japan and Canada for using too many resources.

7 America uses around eight times more of the Earth's resources than Ethiopia.

8 The report says that we must look hard at the way we live if we want to save our planet.

Discussion box

Work in pairs or small groups. Discuss the questions together.

1 Which of the facts in the article do you find most worrying?
2 What other examples of the destruction of the planet can you think of?
3 Are you worried about the future of our planet? Why / Why not?

2 Grammar

Future continuous

(a) **Look at the examples. Then complete the rule. Write *be*, *present participle* or *will*.**

*Experts **will be discussing** the report later this week in Geneva.*

***Will** we really all **be living** on two new planets fifty years from now?*

Rule:
- When we want to talk about things that will be in progress at a specified future time we use the future continuous tense.
- To form the future continuous tense we use _____ followed by _____ and finally the _____ .

Now   50 years from now

We ***will be living*** on two new planets.

Future perfect

(b) **Look at the example sentences and complete the rule. Write *have*, *past participle* or *will*.**

*By 2050 we **will have used up** all of our planet's resources.*

*At this rate the fish **will have died out** completely by 2030.*

Rule:
- When we want to talk about things that will finish some time between now and a specified time in the future we use the future perfect tense.
- To form the future perfect tense we use _____ followed by _____ and finally the _____ .

Now   2030

By 2030 the fish ***will have died out*** completely.

(c) **Complete the sentences using the future continuous or the future perfect.**

1 We will *have used up / be using up* all the Earth's fresh water by the year 2050.
2 Animals like the tiger will probably *have died out / be dying out* completely thirty years from now.
3 I think people will *have lived / be living* much more environmentally friendly lives in the future.
4 Scientists will *have looked / be looking* hard for a solution to this problem over the next few decades.
5 At the current rate we will *have cut down / be cutting down* all the forests by 2050.
6 Politicians will *have discussed / be discussing* this issue at a conference in March.

(d) **One scientist has a solution to the problem. Look at the schedule and write sentences using the prompts. Use the future perfect or future continuous tenses.**

1 During March 2010 / politicians / discuss / the problem.
   During March 2010 politicians will be discussing the problem.
2 By 2013 / politicians / decide on / an undersea policy.
3 In 2020 / engineers / build / homes under the sea.
4 By 2041 / engineers / finish / undersea project.
5 In 2045 / people / live / under the sea.
6 By 2050 / half the world's population / move / to a home under the sea.

2010 – International conferences from 1st to 31st March.	PHASE 1
2012 – Undersea agreements reached.	PHASE 2
2015 – The start of Undersea Homes project.	PHASE 3
2040 – Completion of Undersea Homes project. Start moving people into homes.	PHASE 4
2050 – 50% of the world's population live under the sea.	PHASE 5

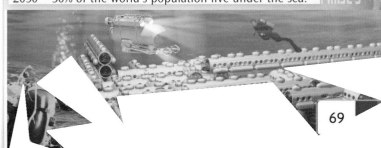

3 Pronunciation

Contracted forms of *will have*

🔊 Turn to page 121.

4 Vocabulary

Global issues

a) Complete the sentences with the words in the box. Then match the underlined phrasal verbs with meanings a–f.

> waste   starvation   species
> temperatures   resources   atmosphere

1   Many _____ of animal are in danger of <u>dying out</u> over the next 50 years.

2   We will soon <u>use up</u> all our natural _____ .

3   We need to find a safe way of <u>getting rid of</u> nuclear _____ .

4   Too many industries are <u>fouling up</u> the _____ without getting punished.

5   Scientists say _____ around the world will <u>go up</u> by as much as 6 per cent over the next century.

6   It's only by helping local people to grow food that we can <u>bring about</u> an end to _____ .

a achieve	d dispose of
b become extinct	e completely finish
c increase	f pollute

b) Work in pairs. Which of the issues in Exercise 4a worries you most? Put the issues in order of importance.

c) Work in small groups. Compare your lists.

5 Listen

a) Work in pairs. Look at the photographs. What do they have in common?

b) 🔊 Listen and number the photographs below in the order they are mentioned. What is the connection between the photographs?

c) 🔊 Listen again and choose a, b, c or d.

1   What do some experts predict we will need to find a replacement for by the year 2010?
      a   cars   b   oil   c   natural resources
      d   energy for offices

2   What can cars with flexible engines run on?
      a   petrol and sugar   b   petrol and alcohol
      c   alcohol and sugar   d   petrol and water

3   Which one of these things do they not do to chicken poo?
      a   heat it   b   turn it into a liquid
      c   add water to it   d   mix it with diesel

4   What does the petrol station use for energy?
      a   solar panels   b   rainwater
      c   birds and fish   d   cars

5   How much energy does the Swiss Re building use compared to conventional buildings?
      a   two thirds as much   b   50 per cent
      c   double   d   the same amount

Wind turbines generate electricity

Rainwater collected from roof used to flush toilets

Solar cells on the roof convert sun's rays into electricity

Pump nozzles designed to stop harmful fuel vapours escaping

6 Vocabulary

Conserving energy

a Look at the poster and complete the sentences with the verbs in the box.

> Take   Switch   Use   Recycle
> Unplug   Swap   Cut down   Wash

You can make a difference – eight ways to save energy

1 .... waste paper.

2 .... on the amount of TV you watch.

3 .... the bus to school (or walk!).

4 .... off the lights when you leave the room.

5 .... your clothes in cold water.

6 .... a microwave oven to cook.

7 .... electrical appliances when you're not using them.

8 .... your conventional light bulbs for long-life ones.

b Make a list of other things you can:

1 switch off?   3 unplug?

2 recycle?   4 cut down on?

c Work in small groups. Discuss the questions.

1 What could you / the school do to reduce the amount of energy you use?

2 In what ways could your town be considered environmentally friendly?

3 What is your government doing to be more 'green'?

4 What ways can you think of to make people more aware of our world's problems?

7 Grammar

Future time expressions

a Complete the sentences with the words in the box.

> ~~by~~   during   for   from now   time   until

a I wouldn't be surprised if we see more petrol stations like this _____*by*_____ the end of the year.

b Hopefully **a few years** _____ we'll be seeing cars like these on the streets of London too.

c Who knows, **in five years'** _____ all our cars might be chicken powered.

d Scientists are going to have to work _____ days if they want to solve this.

e Experts predict we've only got _____ 2010 to find a source of energy to take the place of oil.

f We'll be seeing a lot of changes _____ the next decade.

b Complete the rules. Use *during, until, by* or *for*.

Rule:

- _____ is used to talk about a period of time.

- _____ is used to say how long something will take.

- _____ is used to talk about a future deadline; an action that will be completed <u>before</u> (or at) a specific time.

- _____ is also used to talk about a deadline; the emphasis is on a continuous situation that will stop <u>at</u> a specific time.

Look

The time markers *during, for, by* and *until* can also be used with other tenses.

*I woke up three times **during** the night.*
*I've been waiting **for** an hour.*
*We had to arrive **by** 7pm.*
*We're living here **until** we find a better house.*

8 Speak

Work with a partner. Student B: turn to page 122. Student A: circle the correct time expressions. Then ask your partner the questions. You start.

1 What things have you got to finish *until / by* Friday?

2 Where do you think you'll be *from / in* thirty years' time?

3 What will you be doing *for / during* the next school holidays?

The factory

9 Read and listen

(a) 🔊 **What's the problem with the factory? What idea does Matt like? Read, listen and check your answers.**

Caroline: It's really interesting, this article.

Joanne: What's it about?

Caroline: The pet food factory in Mansfield Road. You know, the one that smells really bad when you walk past it. Well, it says here in the newspaper that the factory's been polluting the river too.

Ash: It's terrible. Someone should do something about it. Maybe *we* should do something about it.

Matt: Us? Come off it! There's nothing we can do!

Joanne: Brilliant! If everyone takes that attitude, then soon there'll be nothing of our Earth left to enjoy. Of course there's something we can do. We just need to get organised.

Matt: OK. Point taken. I never realised you were so ... so ...

Joanne: So what?

Matt: Well, environmentally-minded, I suppose. I thought you were just like the rest of us, you know, ticking along.

Ash: Hang on! Since when do I fit into that category?

Caroline: Well, let's not start arguing amongst ourselves. The point is, what are we going to do about this factory?

Joanne: Right. It's disgusting, that factory. It's really fouling up the atmosphere.

Ash: So, let's start a petition or something. Maybe we could organise a demonstration.

Matt: Now *that* idea I like! We could get some cool banners – you know, 'Youth Against the Factory!' and stuff like that.

Caroline: I know someone who could help us out with the banners and things. Josh Willis at school, he's a neat artist.

Ash: I'm sure he'll help. He's a great guy, Josh.

Joanne: Well, I'm not so sure that he *will* want to help us.

Ash: Oh? Why?

Joanne: Well, I've just remembered. His mother and his brother work at the factory, don't they?

Matt: You're right. And so does my mate Alan's father. I'd almost forgotten.

Caroline: Hmm, that's a problem. We won't be very popular if we try to close the factory.

Matt: In fact, it sounds like a pretty good way to lose a few friends.

Ash: Hey, so what? If the factory's polluting our air, it needs to be closed.

Joanne: Well, actually, I'm not so sure. Read the end of the article. It says: 'The owners of the factory have agreed to repair any damage and to put an end to the pollution.'

(b) **Read again and answer the questions.**

1 In what way does Joanne surprise Matt?

2 What ideas do they mention to protest against the factory?

3 Why do they think they won't be popular if they try to close the factory?

4 Why is Joanne 'not so sure' that the factory needs to be closed?

10 Everyday English

(a) Find expressions 1–5 in the story. Who says them?

1 Come off it!
2 Point taken.
3 stuff like that
4 So what?
5 Since when ...?

Which one means:

a You're right. □
b Why does that matter? □
c That's not true and never has been. □
d Be serious! □
e Other things similar to these. □

(b) Use one of the phrases in each space.

1 He's really into skateboarding, rollerblading and ....

2 A: I think I want to be a racing driver when I leave school.
  B: .... You can't even ride a bike.

3 A: Did you know that there are 700 different types of cheese in England?
  B: .... I've never seen that many cheese packets in the supermarket.

4 A: But if you do a Saturday job, you won't be able to play in the volleyball team.
  B: .... I need the money.

5 A: And you know that if the house is a mess, Dad will never give us a lift to the party.
  B: .... I'll start doing the washing up.

11 Write

(a) Read the article. Is the writer optimistic or pessimistic about the future?

(b) Read the article again. Which of the following areas does the writer cover in his/her text?

- his/her personal situation in 50 years' time from now
- scientists' warnings concerning the Earth's future
- his/her own beliefs about what the future will be like
- peace vs. war
- his/her professional situation in 50 years' time
- the future of the car and other means of transport
- people's life styles
- what people will eat / hunger in the world

(c) Write your own magazine article with the same title. Follow these steps:

- Go through the list of ideas in Exercise 11b. Decide which you would like to include.
- Brainstorm each of the ideas and write down key words.
- Organise your ideas into paragraphs.
- Write a draft of your article. Read it through and check it. Try to improve it. Write a final draft.

OUR LIFE – 50 YEARS FROM NOW

Hurricane in Florida! Deadly forest fires in Portugal! Floods in large parts of China! Hardly a month goes by without headlines that tempt us all to believe that the world will be coming to an end soon. And indeed there are lots of warnings from scientists that the future of the earth will be a gloomy one if we carry on exploiting natural resources and polluting our environment.

But isn't the history of mankind a record of warnings that the end of the world is near? Hasn't man so far been perfectly able to come up with new inventions and ideas that have overcome difficult situations? The answer to these questions can only be yes – and yes it has to be!

So, let's look forward. Exciting times are ahead of us. Over the next decades, the governments of the most powerful countries of the world will learn to accept that our planet needs peace, and the creativity and talent of people from all countries. By the year 2020, the world therefore will be a peaceful place. All the weapons of mass destruction will be destroyed, and the best minds of mankind, men and women, will be working together to find solutions to all the world's problems. By 2040, more than half of the world's population will be living in big cities under the seas. Of course, the water of the oceans will have been cleaned by then, and scientists will have found new fuels that do not pollute the environment. Although the fish in the oceans will have disappeared, new ways of producing food will have been found to prevent starvation.

I am absolutely sure that in 50 years' time from now the world will be a place where people will love to live.

11 Stars step in

* Reduced relative clauses
* Question tags review
* Vocabulary: fame
* Vocabulary: expressing your opinion

1 Read and listen

a) Look at the photos. Do you recognise the people? What do they have in common? Read the text quickly and find out.

Celebrity Ambassadors

Celebrity Ambassadors

☐ In the 1950s, the United Nations first had the idea of using celebrity ambassadors, when they took on Hollywood star Danny Kaye to promote children's rights. Ever since, hundreds of stars, from screen icon Sophia Loren to boxing legend Muhammad Ali, have been seen spreading the word of the international peace organisation at photocalls throughout the world.

☐ Most stars are recruited independently by the various UN agencies. The UN Development Program uses Brazilian footballer Ronaldo to bring attention to the issue of poverty. And the refugee agency UNHCR uses Angelina Jolie, who these days is probably as famous for her humanitarian work as she is for her acting, to highlight the condition of those people left homeless through war.

☐ But perhaps the agency most represented by the rich and famous is UNICEF, the UN children's fund. It has a whole host of stars who act as Goodwill Ambassadors, including singer Ricky Martin and actresses Whoopi Goldberg and Susan Sarandon. There are also celebrities who are used to promote one-off projects every now and then. Pop star Robbie Williams, for example, although not a Goodwill Ambassador, has done several concerts for UNICEF. Of course, it's important that the UN, which has offices in more than 200 countries, is represented by an international mix of celebrities. And many of their most important stars, such as Miss Universe, Mpule Kwelagobe, who was recently appointed Goodwill Ambassador for Botswana, are not household names in the UK.

☐ Choosing the right person must be done extremely carefully. The organisation looks for celebrities who have not only made it big globally, but who are also going to remain famous for many years to come. 'We can't have someone who has just enjoyed success for a few minutes and then disappeared,' says a spokeswoman. Likewise, the star must have already shown a true passion for the cause and they must want to do more than just appear caring in front of the cameras. 'Our celebrities do it because they have real compassion for children,' says the spokeswoman. 'They should have the power to draw the cameras but without wanting the attention for themselves.'

David Beckham is ...

perhaps the world's most famous footballer.

What he does:
Beckham is involved in UNICEF's Sports for Development programme, which promotes the power of sport to improve children's lives.

What he says:
'It is one of the proudest moments of my life to be given the role of UNICEF Goodwill Ambassador and I hope to play a part in supporting these children at their time of need.'

Shakira Mebarak is ...

an international singing sensation.

What she does:
Using her popularity and interest in children's issues, Shakira promotes UNICEF's mission of ensuring the safety of every child around the world.

What she says:
'UNICEF has done tremendous work in my home nation of Colombia. I have seen first-hand the difference UNICEF makes.'

(b) Match the headings A–D with the paragraphs. Write A–D in the boxes.

A   Stars put children first.

B   A few of the familiar faces.

C   More than fifty years of tradition.

D   Not just any star will do.

Discussion box

Work in pairs or small groups. Discuss these questions together.

1   What are the advantages/disadvantages for the UN of having stars involved in their campaigns?

2   What other stars do you know who do charity work?

3   Which famous people in your country would be good as UN Goodwill Ambassadors? Why?

(c) 🔊 Read the texts again and listen. Answer the questions.

1   What role have celebrities played in the UN since the 1950s?

2   What is Angelina Jolie famous for, apart from her acting?

3   What factors are taken into consideration when choosing UN Goodwill ambassadors?

2 Grammar

Reduced relative clauses

(a) Look at the examples. Where could you add the words *that is* and *who are*?

There are also celebrities used to promote one-off projects occasionally.

But perhaps the agency most represented by the stars is UNICEF.

(b) Circle the correct words to complete the rule.

Rule:

● When relative clauses are *passive / active*, we can leave out the relative pronoun and the *verb be / past participle*.

(c) Complete the text about another UNICEF Goodwill Ambassador. Use the words in the box.

> attended   written   who was born   which was given
> held   who is regarded   who was accompanied   won

factfile

UNICEF's latest Goodwill Ambassador is also their youngest. 23-year-old Lang Lang, [1]_____ as the most exciting pianist of our times, will work to bring awareness to the needs of children throughout the world.

Lang Lang, [2]_____ into a musical family in Shenyang, started piano lessons at the age of three. At nine, he entered the Central Music Conservatory of China. As his talent grew, he began to enter competitions. Among the titles [3]_____ by him was first prize at the prestigious Tchaikovsky International Young Musicians' Competition [4]_____ in 1995 in Japan.

In 1997, 15-year-old Lang Lang, [5]_____ by his father, went to the US to study at the Curtis Institute in Philadelphia. In April 2001, Lang Lang made his Carnegie Hall debut, [6]_____ great reviews by the American critics. At the Great Hall of the People in Beijing he gave a concert [7]_____ by an audience of 8,000 people.

A recent article [8]_____ about him in *Teen People* identified him as one of the 'Top Twenty Teens who will change the World'.

(d) ~~Cross out~~ the words in *italics* which are not needed.

1   An appeal *that was* launched by UNICEF is looking to raise $144.5 million for victims of the Asian Tsunami.

2   A TV announcement *that was* made by David Beckham was used to raise money.

3   The English football star, *who* plays for Real Madrid, recorded a video message asking for public support.

3 Vocabulary

Fame

(a) Circle the correct words. Use the text to help you.

Think of someone in your country who:

1   is *famous for / famous by* entertaining children.

2   *made a name for themselves / did a name for themselves* by marrying someone famous.

3   *did it big / made it big* in international cinema.

4   is a *household name / household person* in sport.

5   *enjoyed a lot of success / liked a lot of success* a few years ago but has since disappeared.

6   is a singing *excitement / sensation* for teenagers.

(b) Work in pairs. Think of answers to the questions.

4 Listen

(a) 🔊 Listen to the opinions of Neil and Aisha. Answer the questions.

1 Who is in favour of famous people getting involved in politics? Why?

2 Who is against famous people getting involved in politics? Why?

(b) 🔊 Listen to six more people. Do they have the same opinion as Aisha, Neil or neither? Tick the boxes.

Neil Porter

Aisha Manning

	Same as Aisha	Same as Neil	Neither
Speaker 1	☐	☐	☐
Speaker 2	☐	☐	☐
Speaker 3	☐	☐	☐
Speaker 4	☐	☐	☐
Speaker 5	☐	☐	☐
Speaker 6	☐	☐	☐

(c) 🔊 Listen again. Who says what? Write the number of the speaker next to each sentence. Then decide who the underlined pronouns refer to.

a (......) <u>They</u>'ve formed their opinion already. ....

b (1) <u>They</u> don't really know what they're talking about anyway. *famous people*

c (......) <u>They</u> don't have to agree with the famous person, after all. ....

d (......) <u>These people</u> should stick to what they know. ....

e (......) It's getting harder and harder to tell the difference between <u>them</u>. ....

f (......) Most of <u>them</u> look and sound really old and boring. ....

(d) Whose opinion do you agree with most?

5 Vocabulary

Expressing opinions

(a) Complete the phrases for expressing opinions. Use the words in the box.

| see thought mind opinion concerned ask |

1 To my .... , ...

2 I'd have .... (that) ...

3 As far as I'm .... , ...

4 If you .... me, ...

5 In my .... , ...

6 The way I .... it, ...

(b) What do these expressions mean? Write ✓ (= agree), ✗ (= disagree) or Ø (= neither agree nor disagree).

1 It's not a good idea.

2 I'm all for it.

3 It doesn't (really) matter.

4 It can't be a bad thing.

5 I'm completely against it.

6 I couldn't care less.

(c) Work in groups. Give your opinions about the topics in the box. Try and use some of the expressions in Exercise 5b.

| graffiti   background music in shops advertising on websites   fast food smoking in public places |

Solve the puzzle to win this powerful ZERO supercomputer

CLICK HERE TO ENTER

6 Grammar

Question tags review

a Read the sentences from the listening text. (Circle) the correct question tags.

1 It gets lots of people interested, *does it / doesn't it* ?

2 It can't be a bad thing, *can it / can't it* ?

3 They've formed their opinion already, *haven't they / have they* ?

4 They don't really know what they're talking about, *don't they / do they* ?

5 They aren't going to listen to politicians, *are they / aren't they* ?

6 It's getting harder and harder to tell the difference between them, *is it / isn't it* ?

7 They should leave politics to professional people, *shouldn't they / should they* ?

8 We wouldn't expect to see the prime minister getting involved in music, *wouldn't we / would we* ?

b Complete the rule. Write *positive* and *negative*.

> **Rule:**
> - We often use question tags at the end of statements, to check facts or to make conversation.
> - If the statement is positive we use a .... tag, and if the statement is negative we use a .... tag.
> - If the statement does not have an auxiliary or modal verb, we use *do/does* (present) or *did* (past).

c Complete the tags for these statements.

1 There was a programme on TV about celebrity politicians, ... there?

2 You didn't have the time to sit down and watch it, ... you?

3 It wasn't as boring as the one we saw last week, ... it?

4 The presenter said some really interesting things about the topic, ... she?

5 We would've watched it if we'd known it was on, ... we?

6 We should've recorded it to use for our school project, ... we?

7 I'm sure the teacher will ask us to watch the one next week, ... he?

8 The way I see it, we don't have to listen to celebrities when they talk about politics, ... we?

7 Pronunciation

Intonation in question tags

🔊 Turn to page 121.

8 Speak

a Read the quotations by famous people. Which do you like best? Why?

'You have made people listen. You have made people care, and you have taught us that whether we are poor or prosperous, we have only one world to share. You have taught young people that they do have the power to change the world.'

> Kofi Annan (UN Secretary-General) pays tribute to Bono, November 1999

'It's really very simple, Governor. When people are hungry they die. So spare me your politics and tell me what you need and how you're going to get it to these people.'

> Bob Geldof, co-organiser of Live8

'How I perceive actors getting involved in politics and charities ... they want even more attention for themselves, it's in their nature.'

> Tracey Ullman, British comedienne

b Work in groups. Discuss your opinions of the quotations.

c If you were famous, what message would you like to promote?

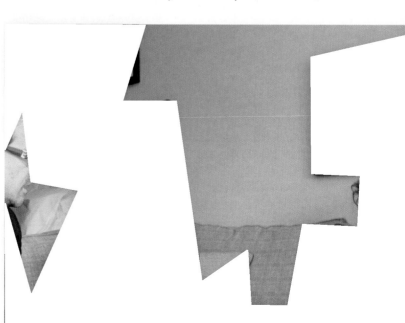

Culture in mind

9 Read

(a) Look at the title. What do you think it means? Read the text quickly and check your guesses.

What is the answer to the question in the title?

Can Music Make a Difference?

On 13th July, 1985 the world was the stage for the largest rock concert it had ever known, Live Aid. This 'global jukebox' was a multi-venue show organised by musicians Bob Geldof and Midge Ure. With main gigs in London's Wembley Stadium and Philadelphia's JFK Stadium, and supporting shows in cities such as Sydney and Moscow, Live Aid had one aim only – to raise as much money as possible for the victims of the famine in Ethiopia.

The shows were a follow-up to the massively successful charity hit single 'Do they know it's Christmas?', which was also the idea of Geldof and Ure and featured many British and Irish artists performing under the name of Band Aid.

Live Aid brought together a host of mainly British and American musicians, past and present, and included such names as Sting, Mick Jagger, The Beach Boys, Elton John, Madonna, Led Zeppelin, U2, Queen, David Bowie, Santana, Duran Duran and Paul McCartney.

Audiences of 72,000 at Wembley and 90,000 in Philadelphia were joined by around 1.5 billion spectators in 100 countries around the world, who watched the shows live on television. Throughout the TV broadcasts, viewers were continually asked to phone up and donate money. The day after, between £40 and £50 million had been raised. It is now estimated that, over time, the Live Aid concerts made around £150 million for the famine relief fund.

Twenty years after Live Aid, in June 2005, Bob Geldof and Midge Ure were once again the instigators behind a series of worldwide concerts, which went under the name of Live 8. This time it was a more international affair. The shows, ten of which were held simultaneously on 2nd July, with one four days later on 6th July in Edinburgh, were held to coincide with the meeting of the heads of the G8 nations in Scotland. This time the aim was not to raise money, but to put pressure on the presidents and prime ministers of the world's richest nations to drop all foreign debt and increase their aid to the world's poorest nations. In order to do this, a huge petition was organised, with people all over the world signing their names via the internet and mobile phone text messages. This was then presented to the world leaders at their meeting. This petition, with currently more than 38 million names, can still be accessed and signed on-line at the official Live8 website.

Many of the artists who performed at the original Live Aid concert returned to play again. They were joined by modern-day stars such as Black Eyed Peas, Alicia Keys, Joss Stone, Green Day and Robbie Williams. Again the shows were watched by millions all over the world on TV.

Whether or not the shows were a success will only be known over the next decades. Promises have been made by World leaders to increase foreign aid and cancel out debt, but it remains to be seen if these will be kept.

(b) Answer the questions Live Aid or Live 8 or both.

1 The concerts were mainly held in the US and the UK.

2 The event was organised by Bob Geldof and Midge Ure.

3 The show was to help starving people in Africa.

4 The concerts were shown on TV.

5 The concerts were held on more than one day.

6 The aim of the event was to apply political pressure.

7 It is not known yet how successful the event was.

Discussion box

Work in pairs or small groups. Discuss these questions together.

1 Which two artists would you most like to see live?

2 What other 'charity' shows do you know of?

3 Do you think shows like these can really make a difference? Why / Why not?

4 If you could organise a show like these, what issue/s would you promote and what acts would you invite to play?

10 Write

(a) Read the composition. What arguments does the writer give for/against politicians becoming media stars?

(b) Read the composition again. Complete it with the words in the box.

> days   same   addition   things   past
> hand   course   but

(c) Which of the expressions 1–8 in the text can be replaced by the expressions below?

a Then again   b At the end of the day
c Years ago   d obviously   e nowadays
f Moreover   g Equally   h finally

(d) Work in pairs. Discuss the writer's opinions. Which do you agree/disagree with? Why? What is your view about the writer's conclusion?

(e) Write your own composition about the topic, *Should pop stars become political?* Follow these steps:

- Think of one or two examples of pop stars who have become political.

- List three arguments in favour of pop stars becoming political, and three arguments against. Make notes.

- Decide what your own opinion is.

- Organise your notes into paragraphs:
  1) introduction; 2) arguments *for*;
  3) arguments *against*; 4) your opinion and conclusion.

- Write a first draft. Try to include some of the linking expressions from Exercise 10c.

- Take a short break, then check your writing.

Should politicians become media stars?

[1] *In the* _____ nobody would have known what the British prime minister had for breakfast, or what the name of the American president's dog was. Many politicians [2] *these* _____ , however, are trying to become media stars, and we learn details of their private lives from chat shows and glossy magazines. Is this a development we should be happy with?

[3] *Of* _____ , there are people who think it is perfectly acceptable that politicians are media stars. They might argue that society has changed, and entertainment is part of our daily lives. If politicians want to be accepted by a large number of people, they need to adapt to our life styles and appear on chat shows, and not just on news programmes. They could also argue that the better we get to know our politicians as humans, and not just as representatives of a political party, the easier it is to decide who to vote for. [4] *In* _____ , politics is about gaining power, and, in a democracy, a politician's ambition must be to gain as much power as possible so that they can have a greater influence on how society is run. If a good politician gets more public support by turning up on chat shows, so be it!

[5] *On the other* _____ , there are lots of arguments against politicians becoming media stars. Although entertainment is certainly part of our daily lives, politics should not be about fun. Politicians need to be serious and professional, and they should focus on their important work, and not be distracted by seeking fame and celebrity status. [6] *In the* _____ *way*, one might argue that people switch on the TV because they want to get away from politics and the problems of their daily lives, and they don't want to see politicians spoiling their favourite TV shows. And [7] *last,* _____ *not least* it can be harmful for the development of a political system if politics becomes mixed up with entertainment. Politics should be about truth and reality, not entertainment, and so there should be strict rules to keep them apart.

[8] *All* _____ *considered,* I personally am not really against politicians becoming media stars because I am not affected by their celebrity personas. In order to decide who to vote for, I try to be well informed by reading newspapers and through discussions with friends who are also seriously interested in politics. I will definitely never be influenced in my decisions by superficial TV programmes!

For your portfolio

12 The global village

* Grammar of phrasal verbs review
* Vocabulary: meanings of phrasal verbs
* Vocabulary: approximate numbers

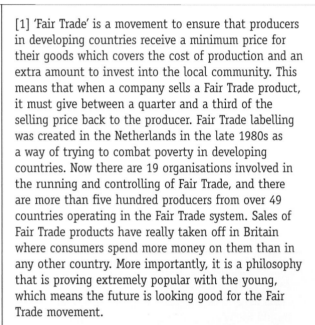

1 Read and listen

(a) Work with a partner. Have you heard of Fair Trade? If so, what do you know about it? If not, what do you think it might be?

(b) Read the text quickly to check your ideas.

[1] 'Fair Trade' is a movement to ensure that producers in developing countries receive a minimum price for their goods which covers the cost of production and an extra amount to invest into the local community. This means that when a company sells a Fair Trade product, it must give between a quarter and a third of the selling price back to the producer. Fair Trade labelling was created in the Netherlands in the late 1980s as a way of trying to combat poverty in developing countries. Now there are 19 organisations involved in the running and controlling of Fair Trade, and there are more than five hundred producers from over 49 countries operating in the Fair Trade system. Sales of Fair Trade products have really taken off in Britain where consumers spend more money on them than in any other country. More importantly, it is a philosophy that is proving extremely popular with the young, which means the future is looking good for the Fair Trade movement.

[2] A recent survey, which looked into British people's attitudes towards 'Fair Trade', found that school and university students in the UK are particularly enthusiastic about the subject. Indeed, nine out of ten students said they wanted to see their schools and universities offer Fair Trade products, such as chocolate, coffee, tea and bananas, in their shops and canteens. Moreover, seven out of ten young people said they would be willing to buy a Fair Trade product even if the price was slightly higher. Although the enthusiasm is there, however, educational establishments are proving slow to accommodate their students' wishes. In fact, the survey suggests that only 8 per cent of schools and universities offer Fair Trade products.

[3] It seems that it is the desire to make a difference to the lives of the poor which is driving young people's consumer choices. Approximately 80 per cent said the main reason they buy Fair Trade goods is to help out the poor. They think it is important that the people who produce the food they eat are paid a fair wage. And it is not just the issue of Fair Trade that interests the young: more than 90 per cent of them said that they wanted to find out what else they could do to change their life style to benefit the poor. Fair Trade products often cost more than non-Fair Trade items, but a lot of people are prepared to put up with slightly higher prices if it improves the lives of workers in developing countries, many of whom find it difficult to get by.

[4] One student at Birmingham University told us: 'When I buy a 60 pence Fair Trade chocolate bar, I know that the money is helping somebody in the developing world to get the wage they deserve. Maybe they'll be able to save up this extra money and send their children to university. The feeling I'm doing something positive makes up for the extra money I spend.'

[5] Unfortunately, the survey showed that far more young people care about Fair Trade than the rest of the public, with roughly 60 per cent of young people recognising the 'Fair Trade' label compared to 20 per cent of the general population. In addition, almost 50 per cent of young people say they buy Fair Trade products on a regular basis, compared to only 5 per cent of the general population. Many adults express the worry that if Fair Trade is not controlled, it might become just another fashion. Big companies might take advantage of consumers' concern and try to get away with selling their 'normal' products under a trendy label. Some older people said they wanted to see new rules and regulations to guarantee real Fair Trade products. For now, at least, it seems to be more difficult to bring older people round to the idea of buying Fair Trade.

Discussion box

Work in pairs or small groups. Discuss these questions together.

1 Do you have Fair Trade products in your country? What type of products?

2 What reasons can you think of for buying or not buying Fair Trade products?

3 Are you prepared to pay slightly more for food so that the producers get fairer prices? Why / Why not?

c 🔊 Read the text again and listen. Write *T* (true) or *F* (false).

1 The Netherlands was the first country to have Fair Trade labels.

2 Fair Trade in the UK has a bright future.

3 90 per cent of young people would like to see Fair Trade products in their school canteens.

4 Most schools and universities are providing their students with the option of buying Fair Trade products.

5 Most young people who buy Fair Trade products do so because they think it's cool.

6 Most young people don't care if the people who produce our food get a fair price or not.

7 Many older people don't really trust the idea of Fair Trade.

8 It is more difficult to persuade older people to buy Fair Trade products than younger people.

2 Grammar

Phrasal verbs review

a Find and underline the phrasal verbs in the text in Exercise 1 which mean:

1 returns (para 1)

2 tolerate (para 3)

3 survive financially (para 3)

4 suddenly increased (para 1)

5 investigated (para 2)

6 discover (para 3)

7 cancels out the bad side (para 4)

8 not get caught (para 5)

9 persuade (para 5)

Rule:

- A With some phrasal verbs, the two parts cannot be separated.
  A recent survey, which looks into young people's attitudes to Fair Trade ...
  (Not: *A recent survey, which looks young people's into attitudes to Fair Trade.*)

- B Other phrasal verbs can be separated, and we can put an object between the two parts.
  The company gives back a third of the money.
  The company gives a third of the money back.
  However, when we use a pronoun with these verbs, we must put it between the two parts of the verbs.
  The company gives it back. (Not: *The company gives back it.*)

- C Some phrasal verbs have three or more parts. These cannot be separated.
  People are prepared to put up with slightly higher prices.

b What type of phrasal verb, A, B or C, are the phrasal verbs in Exercise 2a?

c Put the words in order to make sentences. In one sentence, there is more than one possibility.

1 camera / the / give / back   *Give the camera back* or *Give back the camera* .

2 won't / up / I / with / put / it ....

3 enough / money / to / I've / get / got / by ....

4 the / in / I / looked / word / dictionary / up / my ....

5 make / it / up / didn't / what you said / for ....

6 didn't / bring / to the idea / me / round / she ....

7 the / looking / robbery / into / are / the / police ....

8 found / happened / what / never / we / out ....

3 Vocabulary

Meanings of phrasal verbs

a Phrasal verbs can have more than one meaning. Look at these sentences. What does *take off* mean in each sentence?

1 His acting career had just *taken off* when he was tragically killed in a car crash.

2 He's really good at *taking* me *off*. I mean, he sounds just like me.

3 The plane had a problem as it was *taking off*, and had to return to the airport.

4 The three men were acting very suspiciously and *took off* as soon as the police car arrived.

5 Can you *take* your shoes *off* and leave them by the door.

(**b**) Here are some more phrasal verbs which can have more than one meaning. Complete the pairs of sentences using the correct form of the phrasal verbs in the box.

> make up   come across   bring round
> go up   send off   take back

1 a We didn't really like the idea at first, and it took her a lot of time to _____ us _____ .

   b He was unconscious when they arrived at the hospital, but the doctors managed to _____ him _____ .

2 a There was nothing here 12 months ago. The whole shopping centre _____ in a year.

   b The price of petrol is so expensive! It's _____ four times this year.

3 a When he hit the other player, the referee had no choice but to _____ him _____ .

   b Have you _____ that letter yet? It's really important.

4 a First I want you to _____ what you said, and then I want you to apologise.

   b Every time I hear that song it really _____ me _____ to when I was a teenager.

5 a When you first meet Allan he _____ as a bit shy, but he isn't.

   b I was looking through some old boxes when I _____ my grandmother's diaries.

6 a I don't believe you. I think you're _____ it _____ .

   b They had a terrible argument. I don't think they're ever going to _____ .

4 Read and listen

(**a**) Look at this website. Some of the information is missing.

In groups, discuss what the missing information might be.

(**b**) 🔊 Listen and complete the text with <u>one</u> or <u>two</u> words only.

http://www.thevillageearth.org/thinking.html

THE VILLAGE EARTH

If we could turn the population of the Earth into a small village community of 100 people, keeping roughly the same proportions we have today on our planet, it would be something like this.

Welcome to our Global Village, the village Earth. In our village there are **100** people.

51 people are women and **49** are [1] _____ .

61 people are from [2] _____ .

12 people are from [3] _____ .

14 people are from North and South [4] _____ .

There are **13** people from [5] _____ .

13 people don't have enough to [6] _____ , or are actually dying from hunger.

More than **40** people in the village live without basic sanitation, and **16** people live without water that can be drunk.

Roughly **14** adults in the village can't read or write. Only **seven** have had a secondary school [7] _____ .

Eight people have a computer, and **four** are [8] _____ to the internet.

Eight people have a car each, and **ten** per cent of the houses are powered by electricity.

Some people keep their food in a refrigerator, and their clothes in a ⁹_____ ; they have a roof over their heads, and they have a bed to sleep in. These people represent about **75** per cent of the entire ¹⁰_____ of the village.

Six people in our village own **59** per cent of the entire wealth of all the people in our community.

Forty seven people live on **two** dollars or less a day.

25 people struggle to live on ¹¹_____ a day or less.

If you have a bank account, you're **one** of the **30** ¹²_____ people in the village.

Of all the money that the village spends every year: about **5.5** per cent is spent on weapons and ¹³_____ , roughly **3.4** per cent is spent on ¹⁴_____ and something like **2.6** per cent is spent on keeping people ¹⁵_____ .

Next year, there will be **105** people in the village.

Work with passion,
Love without needing to be loved,
Appreciate what you ¹⁶_____ ,
And do your best for a ¹⁷_____ **world.**

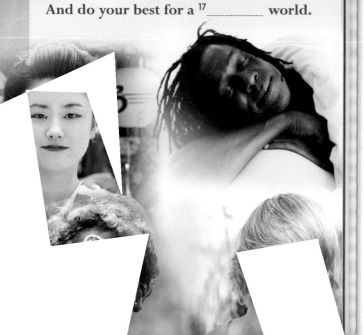

Discussion box

Work in pairs or small groups. Discuss these questions together.

1 Do you think any of the numbers are surprising? If so, which ones?

2 The numbers and percentages keep changing. Which do you think are getting smaller, and which do you think are getting bigger?

5 Pronunciation

Shifting stress

🔊 Turn to page 121.

6 Speak

(a) Work in pairs. Note down as many examples as you can of:

- TV programmes from abroad that are popular in your country
- groups / singers / kinds of music from abroad that are popular in your country
- items of food you eat regularly that are imported from another country
- products you use every day that are made in another country

(b) What percentage of the above come from abroad? Discuss in pairs.

I think that roughly 60 per cent of the TV programmes here are from abroad.

No, it's less than that! If you ask me, it's something like 25 per cent.

7 Listen and speak

(a) Look at the title of the song. What do you think the song will be about? Listen and check your ideas.

(b) 🔊 Listen to the song. The lines in each verse are in the wrong order. Number them as you hear them.

I'd Like to Teach the World to Sing
by The New Seekers

I'd like to build the world a home ....
Grow apple trees and honey bees ....
And snow-white turtle doves ....
And furnish it with love ....

I'd like to hold it in my arms ....
And keep it company ....
In perfect harmony ....
(In perfect harmony) ....
I'd like to teach the world to sing ....
(Sing like me) ....

I'd like to see the world for once ....
And hear them echo through the hills ....
All standing hand in hand ....
(That's the song I hear) ....
Oh, peace throughout the land ....

In perfect harmony ....
I'd like to teach the world to sing ....

Did you know ...?

Famous songs are often used in advertisements, but the idea for this song actually came *from* an advert for Coca-Cola™. The original lyrics were: 'I'd like to buy the world a Coke and keep it company.' It was so popular that in 1971 an Australian band, The New Seekers, reworked the song, and it went straight to the top of the charts in the USA and the UK. The Coca-Cola Company™ gave all their profits from the song – around $80,000 – to UNICEF. A new version of the song was used again in adverts for the soft drink in 2005.

(c) Match words 1–4 with definitions a–d. Use a dictionary.

1 to furnish
2 turtle doves
3 harmony
4 to keep someone company

a small pale-coloured birds that make a soft 'coo' sound
b to stay with someone so that they are not alone
c to supply, or to provide
d a state of peace, when people agree with each other

(d) Answer the questions. Work in pairs.

1 Do you think that music can make people feel more at peace? Could a song stop war?
2 If you could teach everyone in the world a song, what would it be? Give reasons for your choice.

8 Write

Students were asked to carry out a survey among their classmates.

a Read through one student's report on his survey quickly. What was the survey about and was the student surprised by the results?

Home and

Report on a survey carried out in Class 5C at St John's Secondary School.
Date: 5th March

(1) This is a brief report on a survey carried out among the students in my class on the topic of 'Home and abroad'. The survey was aimed at finding out whether students prefer watching TV shows from abroad or from their own country. The survey also investigated students' choices of music, food, everyday products and the clothes they wear.

(2) More than 70 per cent of the students interviewed said that they think TV shows from their own country are better than the ones from abroad. The majority of the students, however, prefer listening to music from abroad. Only a small minority of the students (about 15 per cent) said that they regularly eat food from abroad, but approximately half of the students said they would like to eat more local food. Approximately half of the students think that at home they use more products from abroad, and something like 60 per cent wear clothes that were made in other countries.

(3) A number of students made very interesting comments. A typical answer was "I don't really care whether something is from my own country or from abroad. What's more important for me is the price and the quality of what I buy." Only one student said that he always chooses things from his own country and claimed that this was an important principle for him.

(4) I must say that I was not at all surprised by the outcome of the survey. The answers I got were in line with my own thoughts on the subject, but nevertheless it was very interesting to carry out the survey because it backed up what I had expected.

b Read the report again. Match headings A–D with paragraphs 1–4.

- A Report of the key findings from the survey.
- B The reporter's own opinion.
- C Introduction: what was the survey about?
- D Examples of students' comments.

c Read the report again and:

1 Underline two expressions that are used to say what the survey wanted to learn (paragraph 1).
2 Underline the expressions that are used to talk about approximate numbers (paragraph 2).
3 Find words which mean:
   a result (paragraph 4)
   b similar to (paragraph 4)
   c confirmed (paragraph 4)

d Does the student use reported or direct speech or both to talk about some of the comments the students made?

e Write down the questions that you think the student asked his/her classmates.

f Carry out a survey in your class on the use of the internet. Follow these steps:

- In groups, write up a list of questions you want to ask your classmates. Choose questions that are most likely to get interesting answers.
- Ask and answer the questions in class. Take notes and calculate the approximate percentages.
- Carry out individual interviews to get personal comments. Take notes.
- Write your report (not more than 300 words). Use the report in Exercise 8a to help you. Make sure you give a good overview of the different opinions. Include interesting comments and your personal opinion. Try to use some of the expressions in Exercise 8c.

For your portfolio

Module 3 Check your progress

1 Grammar

a Complete the conditional sentences.

1 If I hadn't had a big lunch I _would be_ (be) hungry now.
2 If I spoke French I .... (get) the job.
3 If she doesn't pass her driving test this time, she .... (give up) driving.
4 If I'd had enough money I .... (buy) the bigger bike.
5 I .... (go) to the club if I liked dancing.
6 I wouldn't be tired if the dog .... (bark) all night.

☐ 5

b Complete the sentences using the future perfect or the future continuous form of the verb in brackets.

1 They will _have lived_ (live) here for 25 years in May.
2 Don't phone me before nine. I'll .... (do) my homework until then.
3 At this time next week I'll .... (fly) first class to New York.
4 I hope I'll .... (finish) all my work by Friday evening.
5 I'll be OK. Scientists will .... (discover) a 'cure' for old age by the time I'm 50.
6 Have a great birthday tomorrow. I'll .... (think) of you.
7 By the time the film finishes, you'll .... (fall) asleep.

☐ 6

c Complete the sentences with the words in the box.

during	until	~~time~~	by	for	from now

1 I'll finish school in six months' _time._
2 They kept talking .... the film. It was really annoying.
3 Where have you been? I've been waiting .... hours.
4 Ten years .... I'll be married with three children.
5 We've got .... Friday to finish the project.
6 I want you to tell me your answer .... Sunday evening at the latest.

☐ 5

d ~~Cross out~~ the words in *italics* if they are not needed.

1 The gymnast ~~*who is*~~ awarded the most points wins the gold medal.
2 The letter, *that* arrived this morning, had bad news.
3 The concert, *which was* held in Manchester, was attended by 5 million people.
4 The 57-year-old man, *who was* last seen at the train station, is wanted by the police.
5 The man *who* attacked me was wearing a black jacket.
6 The team *that* played the best won the match.

☐ 5

e Complete the sentences with question tags.

1 It was lucky we got tickets because that was a great concert last night, _wasn't it_ ?
2 You can come to my eighteenth birthday party, ... ?
3 She didn't phone you about the time change for tomorrow's dance lesson, ... ?
4 You would tell me if there was anything wrong, ... ?
5 Dave's family are moving to a new town, ... ?
6 You won't tell the teacher that I forgot my homework, ... ?
7 You're new round here, but you go to the same school as me, ... ?

☐ 6

f Put the words in order to make sentences. There is sometimes more than one possibility.

1 camera / the / give / back _Give the camera back_ or _Give back the camera._
2 take / you / come / in / your / shoes / when / off
3 I / come / didn't / kitchen / across / your / glasses / in / the

4 the / in / I / looked / phone / address / book / up / the

5 worry / you / don't / make / can / up / it / for / later

6 the idea / eventually / brought / to / me / round / she

7 looking / a new theatre / into / are / the possibility of building / teachers

☐ 6

2 Vocabulary

a (Circle) the correct preposition to complete the sentences.

1 The Giant Panda is in danger of dying *in / over / out* unless we do something now.

2 I can't believe it. You've used *up / over / on* all my printer ink.

3 You've had that bike since you were ten. It's time you got rid *of / out / off* it.

4 That factory is really fouling *in / up / down* the air in this town.

5 My maths grades have gone *up / above / over* from 56% to 78%!

☐ 5

b Use the clues to complete the puzzle.

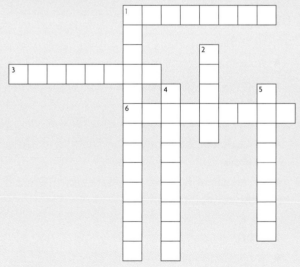

Across

1 This is an amount of money which you decide to give to a charity.

3 This is a document which many people sign to ask governments or companies for action about an important problem.

6 This adjective describes an activity, e.g. a marathon or a long walk, which raises money for charity.

Down

1 This is when a lot of people get together in a public place to protest about something. They often hold signs and shout about whatever they want to change.

2 This is another way to say 'get' money for charity.

4 If you do this type of work, you don't get paid.

5 These are paper brochures, usually only one or two pages. People hand them out in the street, often to advertise things.

☐ 7

c Complete each sentence using a word from the box. (There is one word you won't use.)

sensation   for   enjoyed   name   big   household

1 He's more famous .... his lifestyle than his talent.

2 She's made a .... for herself as a tough interviewer of world leaders.

3 Although he's Spanish, he's made it .... in Hollywood.

4 *Spandax 4* are not exactly a .... name in popular music, are they?

5 They .... a bit of success in the 90s but then they disappeared.

☐ 5

d Put the words in order to make expressions to give your opinion.

1 as / as / concerned / I'm / far
   ...*as far as I'm concerned*...

2 all / I'm / it / for

3 less / I / care / couldn't

4 doesn't / it / matter / really

5 it / a / thing / be / bad / can't

6 it / I'm / against / completely

7 a / idea / good / it's / not

☐ 6

How did you do?

Tick (✓) a box for each section.

Total score:	☺	😐	☹
☐ 56	Very good	OK	Not very good
Grammar	25 – 33	17 – 24	less than 17
Vocabulary	18 – 23	12– 17	less than 12

YOU WILL LEARN ABOUT ...

- A very different kind of language ....
- Different accents and dialects in English ....
- A dangerous trip in the Grand Canyon ....
- Using films to make people feel better ....
- Choosing the music we hear in different places ....
- Musical instruments around the world ....

* Can you match each picture with a topic?

YOU WILL LEARN HOW TO ...

Speak

- Talk about disappearing languages
- Talk about regional accents and dialects
- Compare natural and man-made 'wonders of the world'
- Retell part of a story
- Describe an interesting or memorable trip
- Discuss which films would be most suitable for various people
- Talk about the influence that music has on you and other people
- Compare your feelings about different kinds of music

Write

- A narrative about a misunderstanding concerning language
- A description of a place: physical and why you like it
- A discursive essay about a film that you particularly like
- A 'haiku' or 'mini-saga'

Read

- An article about a different language on an island near Spain
- An extract from a modern novel
- Three short texts about wonderful places in the world
- A magazine article about using films to help people
- An article about Bollywood, the film industry in India
- An article about the importance of the music around us all the time

Listen

- A discussion about regional accents and how important they are in our lives
- A story about a dangerous trip in the Grand Canyon
- A discussion about films by Stephen Soderbergh
- A radio programme about musical instruments around the world
- A song about music

Use grammar

Can you match the names of the grammar points with the examples?

Passive report structures   We had **such a good time that** we decided to go back next year.

Participle clauses   Could you tell me **where this instrument comes from**?

Clauses of purpose   I have no idea **where they are** right now.

Result clauses   **Smiling**, the man walked towards me.

Verbs + *wh* clauses   He **is believed to be** in Brazil.

Indirect questions   They phoned the police **in order to** get help.

Use vocabulary

Can you think of two more examples for each topic?

Understanding Language	Geographical features	Reacting to films	Music
catch the gist	valley	cry	lyrics
understand everything	waterfall	laugh	instrumental
....	....	....	....
....	....	....	....

13 Language

* Passive report structures
* Vocabulary: verbs for describing noises people make
* Vocabulary: understanding language

1 Read and listen

(a) How many different ways of communicating can you think of?

(b) Read the article quickly and find out:

1 where Juan Cabello lives;
2 what unusual way of communicating they use there;
3 what is being done to preserve this way of communicating.

Near-Extinct Language Returns
By SARAH ANDREWS

Juan Cabello takes pride in not using a mobile phone or the internet to communicate. Instead, he whistles. Cabello, 50, is a *silbador*, until recently a dying breed on tiny, mountainous La Gomera, one of Spain's Canary Islands off West Africa. Like his father and grandfather before him, he knows 'Silbo Gomero', a language that is whistled, not spoken, and can be heard more than two miles away. This unusual way of communicating is said to have arrived with early African settlers 2,500 years ago. Now, educators are working hard to save it from extinction by making school children study the language up to the age of fourteen.

Silbo, which comes from the Spanish *silbar* (meaning to whistle), features four 'vowels' and four 'consonants' that can be used to form more than 4,000 words. 'I use it for everything: to talk to my wife, to tell my kids something, to find a friend if we get lost in a crowd,' Cabello says. In fact, he makes a living from *Silbo*, performing daily exhibitions at a restaurant on this island of 220 square kilometres and 19,000 people.

People throughout La Gomera are known to have used *Silbo* in the past as a way of communicating over long distances. A strong whistle saved farmers from trekking over the hills to give messages or news to neighbours. Then came the phone. Nowadays, it's hard to know how many people still use *Silbo*. In 1999, it was introduced as a compulsory subject in La Gomera's primary schools, in an effort to prevent the language from becoming extinct. Now 3,000 students are studying it, but only a few people are believed to be able to communicate fully in the whistling language. '*Silbo* is said to

be the most important cultural heritage we have,' said Moises Plasencia, the director of the Canary Islands' government's historical heritage department.

It might seem appropriate for a language that sounds like birdsong to exist in the Canary Islands, but there is thought to be no connection between the islands' name and the birdsong-like way of communicating. In fact, little is known about *Silbo*'s origins. *Silbo*-like whistling has been found in parts of Greece, Turkey, China and Mexico, but none is as developed as *Silbo Gomero*. One study is looking for signs of *Silbo* in Venezuela, Cuba and Texas, all places to which Gomerans have emigrated in the past during hard economic times.

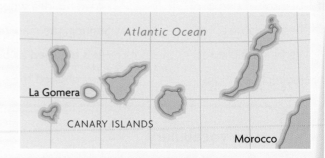

Now, Plasencia is heading an effort to get UNESCO to declare it a 'cultural heritage' and to support efforts to save it. '*Silbo* is so unique, and it has many historical and linguistic values,' he said. And, as Cabello explains, 'It's good for just about anything except for romance: everyone on the island would hear what you're saying!'

Did you know ...?

Worldwide, there are about 7,000 different languages. Every fortnight, a language becomes extinct.

c 🔊 Read the text again and listen. Answer the questions.

1 Where is La Gomera?

2 What theory is there about how *Silbo* came to La Gomera?

3 Why did farmers use *Silbo* in the past?

4 How many people use *Silbo* nowadays and what do they use it for?

5 Is there a connection between the Canary Islands' name and the sound of the language?

6 Why do some people think that they might find *Silbo* in Venezuela, Cuba and Texas?

7 In what way is Moises Plasencia trying to save *Silbo*?

8 What do people not use *Silbo* for, and why?

Discussion box

Work in pairs or small groups. Discuss these questions together.

1 Are there any languages in your country that are dying out? Do you think efforts should be made to save them? Why / Why not?

2 Would you like to learn a language like *Silbo*? Why / Why not?

2 Grammar

Passive report structures

a Find and underline sentences in the text which mean:

1 Experts believe that only a few people can communicate in *Silbo*.

2 Experts think that there is no connection between *Silbo* and the name 'Canary Islands'.

3 Experts say that *Silbo* arrived with African people.

4 Experts know that people in La Gomera used *Silbo* in the past to communicate.

b Complete these sentences from the text.

1 Only a few people _____ able to communicate fully in the whistling language.

2 There _____ no connection between the islands' name and the birdsong-like way of communicating.

3 This unusual way of communicating _____ with early African settlers 2,500 years ago.

4 People throughout La Gomera _____ *Silbo* in the past as a way of communicating over long distances.

c Compare the sentences in Exercise 2a with the sentences in the text. What difference is there in the form of the verbs *know*, *believe* and *think*?

d Which of the sentences talks about

● beliefs or knowledge about the present?

● beliefs or knowledge about the past?

e Rewrite the following sentences using passive report structures.

1 Experts think children are the best language learners.

Children *are thought to be* the best language learners.

2 People say Chinese is a difficult language to learn.

Chinese _____ a difficult language to learn.

3 Experts know some languages disappear every year.

Some languages _____ every year.

4 Experts believe whistling languages exist in other countries.

Whistling languages _____ in other countries.

5 People say the words for *finger* and *toe* are the same in some languages.

The words for *finger* and *toe* _____ the same in some languages.

6 People know French and Latin influenced the English language.

French and Latin _____ the English language.

7 Experts believe many European languages originated in India.

Many European languages _____ in India.

8 Experts say hundreds of languages have died out in the past.

Hundreds of languages _____ in the past.

3 Pronunciation

Words ending in *-ough*

🔊 Turn to page 121.

4 Listen

(a) 🔊 Listen to the beginning of a TV programme. Draw lines between the accents and the cities where they are spoken.

(b) 🔊 Listen again. What examples are given of:

1 pronunciation differences (accent)?
2 vocabulary differences (dialect)?

Look

	foreign	
	regional	
a	London	accent
	heavy	
	strong	
	slight	

(c) 🔊 Listen to the next part of the TV programme. You are going to hear four teenagers talking about their accents. Where do they come from?

Brummie
Scouse
Geordie
Mancunian
Estuary English
Glaswegian

SCOTLAND

Glasgow

Newcastle

IRELAND

Liverpool

Manchester

Birmingham

WALES   ENGLAND

London

Marie

Patrick

Tina

John

(d) 🔊 Write the names. Listen again and check.

1 .... had a small problem at school.
2 .... is not very concerned about his accent.
3 .... isn't going to change how she speaks.
4 .... thinks she didn't get a job in the past because of her accent.
5 .... thinks she wouldn't have got a job in the past because of her accent.
6 .... was not completely understood in London.
7 .... thinks he could lose his accent in the future.
8 .... thinks accents aren't very important these days.

Discussion box

Work in pairs or small groups. Discuss the questions together.

1 Are there many different accents in your country?

2 Are there any accents that you really like (in your own language or in English)? Why?

3 When you meet someone for the first time, can you tell where they come from by their accent?

5 Vocabulary

Understanding language

a 🔊 (Circle) the correct option. Then listen and check.

1 They don't speak English, so of course they didn't understand a *word / sentence* of what I said.

2 He spoke so fast, we just couldn't understand anything. It was *not / totally* incomprehensible!

3 Sorry, could you repeat what you just said? I didn't *miss / catch* it.

4 He's speaking so quietly that I can't *make / do* out anything at all.

5 I *got / listened* some of what she said, but I certainly didn't understand everything.

6 My German is so poor now, that I managed to pick a few words *out / in* but that was all.

7 I got the *part / gist* of it – you know, the general meaning – but no details at all.

8 I don't understand computers, so he *lost / missed* me completely after about two sentences!

b Complete the table with the words in the box.

word   gist   catch   lost   pick

+ understood got caught managed to pick out	everything a lot (of it / of what they said) the .... some of it / of what she said a few words
– couldn't .... out didn't .... didn't get didn't understand	very much a .... (of it / of what they said) anything (at all)
– He/She .... me completely. It was totally incomprehensible.	

c Complete the dialogues. Use the correct form of the verbs from Exercise 5b. Sometimes there is more than one possibility.

1 A: Did they enjoy your talk?
   B: I don't think so. I don't think they .... a word of what I said.

2 A: What's he saying now?
   B: I don't know. It's too noisy in here. I .... anything at all.

3 A: Did you understand the lesson?
   B: I think so. Well, I .... she said. But not everything.

4 A: I really didn't understand that. My German isn't good enough.
   B: Nor mine. I managed to .... , but that's all.

5 A: Wow! That talk was difficult to understand.
   B: It was. I .... – I mean, he was talking about science – but that's all!

6 A: Did you understand him?
   B: No! He .... from the very beginning!

d What do you think the people in the cartoon might be saying?

6 Listen and speak

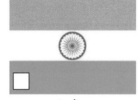

India   Australia

Canada   Jamaica

a 🔊 You are going to hear four people speaking English in their national accents. What country do you think they are from? Number the countries 1–4.

b 🔊 Listen again and make a brief note of what each speaker talks about.

c Work in pairs or groups. Compare answers. Then discuss the four speakers' accents. How much did you understand? Use expressions from Exercise 5b to help you.

'I got the gist of what the person from India was saying.'

'Yes, she's/he's got a strong accent but I managed to pick a few words out.'

'The person from Australia was easier – I understood almost everything!'

Literature in mind

7 Read

(a) Work in pairs. Do you remember any words that you misunderstood when you first heard them as a child? Tell your partner.

(b) Find out what the word *undertow* means. Use a dictionary or ask your teacher.

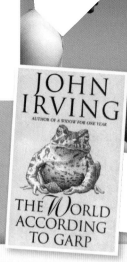

The World According to Garp

by John Irving

This is the story of T. S. Garp, a novelist whose life is a series of happy and tragic events. Son of the famous Jenny Fields, who is murdered, Garp is married to Helen and has two sons, Duncan and Walt. As Garp's fortunes go up and down, we follow him on his roller-coaster ride of life, love, anger, betrayal and laughter.

Duncan began talking about Walt and the undertow – a famous family story. For as far back as Duncan could remember, the Garps had gone every summer to Dog's Head Harbor, New Hampshire, where the miles of beach in front of Jenny Fields' estate were ravaged by a fearful undertow. When Walt was old enough to venture near the water, Duncan said to him – as Helen and Garp had, for years, said to Duncan – 'Watch out for the undertow.' Walt retreated, respectfully. And for three summers, Walt was warned about the undertow. Duncan recalled all the phrases.

'The undertow is bad today.'

'The undertow is strong today.'

'The undertow is *wicked* today.' *Wicked* was a big word in New Hampshire – not just for the undertow.

And for years, Walt reached out for it. From the first, when he asked what *it* could do to you, he had only been told that it could pull you out to sea. It could suck you under and drown you and drag you away.

It was Walt's fourth summer at Dog's Head Harbor, Duncan remembered, when Garp and Helen and Duncan observed Walt watching the sea. He stood ankle-deep in the foam from the surf and peered into the waves, without taking a step, for the longest time. The family went down to the water's edge to have a word with him.

'What are you doing, Walt?' Helen asked.

'What are you looking for, dummy?' Duncan asked him.

'I'm trying to see the Under Toad,' Walt said.

'The what?' said Garp.

'The Under Toad,' Walt said. 'I'm trying to *see* it. How big is it?'

And Garp and Helen and Duncan held their breath; they realized that all these years Walt had been dreading a giant *toad*, lurking offshore, waiting to suck him under and drag him out to sea. The terrible Under Toad.

Garp tried to imagine it with him. Would it ever surface? Did it ever float? Or was it always down under, slimy and bloated and ever-watchful for ankles its coated tongue could snare? The vile Under Toad.

Between Helen and Garp, the Under Toad became their code-phrase for anxiety. Long after the monster was clarified for Walt ('Under*tow*, dummy, not Under Toad!' Duncan had howled), Garp and Helen evoked the beast as a way of referring to their own sense of danger. When the traffic was heavy, when the road was icy – when depression had moved in overnight – they said to each other, 'The Under Toad is strong today.'

'Remember,' Duncan asked on the plane, 'how Walt asked if it was green or brown?'

Both Garp and Duncan laughed.

(c) Read the text and answer the questions.

1 What was dangerous about the beach at Dog's Head Harbor?

2 What was Walt looking for at the water's edge?

3 How long was it before Walt's family realised he had misunderstood?

4 When did Garp and Helen use the expression Under Toad?

Discussion box

Work in pairs or small groups. Discuss these questions.

1 Which adjective would you use to describe the extract: *happy? funny? sad? scary? or your own adjective?*

2 What other things do you think mothers and fathers typically warn their young children about?

3 Can you remember any funny stories from your own childhood? Tell your partner/s.

Misunderstandings

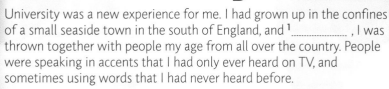

University was a new experience for me. I had grown up in the confines of a small seaside town in the south of England, and ¹_____ , I was thrown together with people my age from all over the country. People were speaking in accents that I had only ever heard on TV, and sometimes using words that I had never heard before.

I had only been at university for about a week when I met Dave Pitman, from Blackburn in the north of England. We discovered that we both played tennis, and arranged to meet up one afternoon for a game.

I went to the sports hall at the time we'd agreed, and went into the changing rooms. Dave was already there, and ²_____ I could see that he wasn't very happy. He was searching ³_____ for something inside his bag. He looked up at me as I walked in.

'I've forgotten my keks,' he said. 'You haven't got any, have you?'

⁴_____ I had no idea what he was talking about. Tennis balls? Shorts? Trainers? What? ⁵_____ I said: 'Sorry?' Dave repeated: 'Have you got any spare keks with you?'

Of course, I could ⁶_____ have asked him what the word meant, but I was too embarrassed and didn't want to offend him. ⁷_____ Dave saw the look on my face, and said: 'You know – keks. Shorts. Tennis shorts.'

Now I understood, and luckily, I did have some shorts in my bag. I lent them to him, we played, and he won. Then we went to get a drink. The woman at the canteen asked me what I wanted. 'I'd like a Black Beauty, please,' I said. (Where I come from, that's cola and ice-cream.) 'What on earth is that?' said the woman. I knew ⁸_____ how she felt.

8 Write

a Read the story and look at the pictures. Which two pictures are not part of the story?

b Which two words / expressions were misunderstood? What do each of them mean in 'standard' English?

c Fill in the spaces with these adverbs / adverbial phrases. There is often more than one possibility.

> in a panic   exactly
> unfortunately   suddenly
> desperately   immediately
> easily   fortunately

d Write a story, between 150 and 250 words, with the title: *A misunderstanding.*

Use an incident that happened to you, or make up a story, where there is/was a misunderstanding due to language (a foreign language, or the same language).

Use adverbs / adverbial phrases to make your story as lively as possible.

①

②

③

④

⑤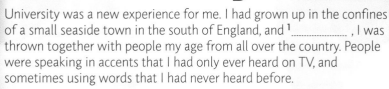

⑥

14 The wonders of the world

* Participle clauses
* *Didn't need to* vs. *needn't have*
* Vocabulary: natural wonders
* Vocabulary: travel verbs

1 Read and listen

(a) Match the names with the photos. What do you know about these things?

> The Northern Lights
> The Great Barrier Reef
> Victoria Falls

(b) Read the texts quickly.

Where do you think they come from? Write 1–3 in the boxes.

1 a travel guide   3 a work of fiction
2 a travel blog

(c) Read the texts again and:

1 Underline three facts about the Great Barrier Reef (text 1).

2 Underline three different types of noise (text 2).

3 Fill in the gaps with the phrases in the box (text 3).

> above the horizon   commonly known
> a must   considered to be

(d) 🔊 Listen and check.

☐ Tomorrow is the day I've been waiting for the most since I started out on this adventure around the world. We arrived in Cairns at midday and, having checked in at the youth hostel, I rushed straight out to book myself on a snorkelling tour of the Great Barrier Reef. Yes, the Great Barrier Reef! It's been a dream of mine for as long as I can remember – swimming with whale sharks and great white sharks too. (OK, perhaps not the great white!) Anyway, I'm booked in with Dundee Reef Adventures who seem very professional. I even got a leaflet with a short history and description of the reef. It's considered the longest of the world's natural wonders, 2,000 km in total, although I don't imagine I'll be swimming the whole length tomorrow! It's made up of the skeletons of marine polyps (whatever they are) that lived and died just under the surface of the ocean. Of course, these days, pollution and man-made damage are the biggest threat to the reef, and conservation is extremely important. That's all for now. Tomorrow I promise a full account of my day on the reef.

☐ For days, the small boat had sailed down the gentle waters of the Zambezi. It was so quiet that at times they felt like the only two men left on the face of the Earth. Just them, the chug of their small engine, and the occasional screech of the parrots as they left the tree-tops and flew downriver. That's why on this morning both men felt that something had changed. At first, neither of them could quite decide what it was and so they didn't talk about it. But after an hour, it had grown so loud that neither man could ignore it any more. For it was a noise which, although it had started out as almost 'invisible', had grown into a loud roar shouting its danger. This huge and gentle river was about to thunder down a huge cliff and they had very little time to do much about it.

☐ Stretching across the skies above the North Pole, the *aurora borealis* amazes visitors to the area, and has done so for centuries. The Northern Lights, as they are more ¹_____, are an ever-changing dance of light and colour, spectacular enough to take anyone's breath away.

In Medieval Europe they were ²_____ heavenly warriors fighting each other. Some people saw them as the bringers of death, illness or even war. These days, of course, scientists have revealed their mystery. The lights are caused by small particles in a solar wind interacting with the Earth's magnetic field. They start as a small dim glow ³_____, and grow until they fill the night sky with dramatic, phosphorescent colour. The result is one of nature's most wonderful shows and ⁴_____ for anyone travelling through Scandinavia.

2 Grammar

Participle clauses

(a) Look at the examples. For each sentence, say *who* or *what* is the subject of both verbs.

A *Stretching across the skies, the aurora borealis amazes visitors.*

B *Having checked in at the hostel, I rushed out to book a tour.*

(b) Match sentences 1–2 with the meanings a–b. Then complete the rule. Write *present* or *perfect*.

1 Reading the letter, I was very nervous.

2 Having read the letter, I was very nervous.

a I felt nervous after I finished reading the letter.

b I felt nervous at the same time that I was reading the letter.

> **Rule:**
> - We use a .... participle (the *-ing* form of the verb) when the action happens or happened at the same time as the main action.
> - We use the present participle of *have* + ... participle when the action happened before the main action.

(c) Join the two sentences to make one. Use participle clauses.

1 I was swimming past a rock. I saw a shark in the distance.

   Swimming past a rock, I saw a shark in the distance.

2 We saw the show. Then we walked slowly back to our hotel.

3 David Livingstone discovered the falls. He named them after the Queen of England.

4 The visitors look up at the sky. All they see are wonderful lights.

5 The water falls 100m into the Batoka Gorge. It makes an incredible noise.

6 The lights flash for hours. Then they disappear.

7 The men listened to the sounds of nature. They felt very alone.

3 Vocabulary

Geographical features

(a) 🔊 Match the words with the pictures. Write 1–10 in the boxes. Then listen and check.

1 a coral reef
2 a bay
3 a lake
4 a canyon
5 a waterfall
6 a mountain range
7 a cliff
8 a plain
9 a glacier
10 a desert

(b) Work in pairs. You have three minutes to think of as many famous examples of these features as you can.

4 Speak

There are many different lists of the seven wonders of the world. Work in pairs. Make your own lists of the:

1 seven *natural* wonders of the world.

2 seven *man-made* wonders of the world.

Look

The subject of the participle clause and the main clause <u>must be the same</u>.

Walking down the street, the sun was shining. ✗

This would mean the sun was walking down the street!

Walking down the street, the boy kicked a stone. ✓

The boy was walking down the street and the boy kicked the stone.

These clauses are more common in writing than in speaking.

5 Listen

a Look at the photos. What do you know about the Grand Canyon? What do you think are the dangers of hiking in the Grand Canyon?

b 🔊 Listen to the first part of the story. Put the sentences in the correct order.

1 They wanted to go down a path called the Bright Angel Trail.

2 After reaching Indian Garden Campground they decided to go on to the Plateau Point.

3 Christine and her friends walked along the rim of the canyon.

4 When they looked down into the canyon, they felt really small.

5 They were given several warnings.

6 They set off early and the hike seemed easy.

c Join the two parts of the warnings.

1	You need to set	a	your hike carefully.
2	You need to plan	b	two days for the whole trip.
3	You need to make	c	off really early.
4	You need to take	d	sure you don't go too far in a day.

d 🔊 Listen to the second part of the story. Take notes. Work with a partner. Take turns to retell the story.

6 Grammar

didn't need to / needn't have

a Look at the examples from the story and answer the questions.

The people at the lodge didn't need to tell us to take a map – we're not stupid!

We needn't have taken our mobile phones – they don't work in the canyon.

1 Was it necessary for the people at the lodge to tell them to take a map?

2 Did they take their mobile phones with them?

b Complete the rule. Write *did something / didn't do something*.

> **Rule:**
> - When we use *didn't need to (do something)*, it often means that someone .... because it was not necessary.
> - When we use *needn't have (done something)*, it means that someone .... but in fact it was not necessary.

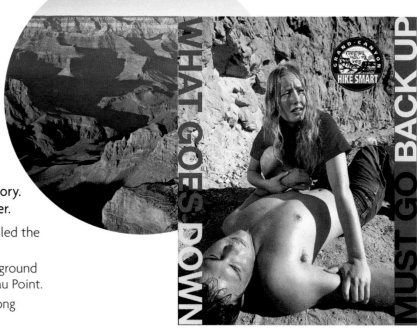

c Complete the sentences with the phrases in the box.

> didn't need to buy   needn't have bought
> didn't need to phone   needn't have phoned
> ~~didn't need to take~~   needn't have taken

1 The doctor said my cold wasn't serious, so I *didn't need to take* any medicine.

2 I took my umbrella on the walk, but the sun shone the whole time, so I .... it.

3 I bought a new coat, but I .... it because my old one was really OK.

4 I managed to do all the homework by myself so I .... any of my friends to help me.

5 I called Wendy to tell her about the party, but I .... her because she already knew.

6 I was going to buy a new camera but I .... one in the end, because my parents gave me one for my birthday.

d Complete the sentences with the verb in brackets. Use *needn't have* where possible. Otherwise, use *didn't need to*.

1 I was nervous about the exam, but I .... (worry) – it was easy!

2 I .... (get up) early yesterday, so I stayed in bed until 11 o'clock.

3 I took my coat with me, but I .... (take) it because it wasn't cold.

4 Thanks for the flowers, but you .... (bring) them.

5 The door was unlocked, so I .... (use) my key.

6 I asked him a question in an email, and I .... (wait) very long – he replied in thirty seconds.

7 Vocabulary

Travel verbs

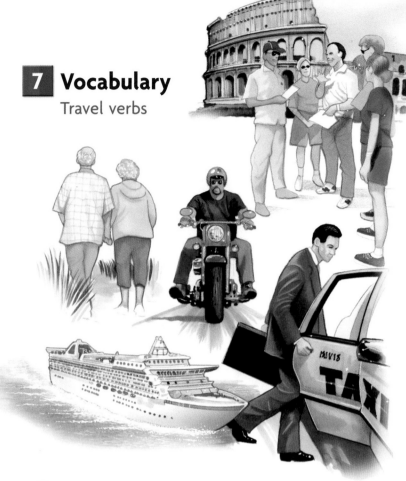

(a) Complete the sentences from the listening text in Exercise 5.

1 I hear you went _____ holiday to the Grand Canyon.
2 They told us to set _____ early.
3 We only got _____ to the lodge at midnight.

(b) Complete the table of travel verbs with the words in the box.

holiday   home   car   flight   taxi   bicycle

go for	a walk a ride (on a bicycle / a motorbike / a horse) a drive (in a car)
go on	a trip / a journey a cruise 1 _____ a tour
go away get get back get in / out of get on / off	for the weekend / for a few days there / to [London] 2 _____ / to [the hotel] a car / a 3 _____ a plane / a bus / a boat / a 4 _____ / a motorbike / a horse
leave for set off take off drive off ride off	= start a trip/journey to a place = start a trip / a journey = start a 5 _____ = start a journey by 6 _____ = start a journey on a bicycle / a motorbike / a horse

(c) In each space write the correct verb in the correct form.

1 She ___got in___ her car and _____ off.
2 Yesterday we _____ for a really long walk. We _____ off at eight and _____ back at four.
3 Last week we _____ on a trip to New York. The plane _____ off at 6 pm and we _____ there at four the next morning.
4 He _____ on his motorbike and _____ off.
5 A: Where are you _____ on holiday this year?
   B: Well, we might _____ on a cruise to Norway.
6 When we _____ to Rome, there was a guided tour of the city but we decided not to _____ on it.
7 A: Have you got any plans for the weekend?
   B: Yes, we're _____ for a couple of days.
8 I love the ending of western films, when the hero _____ on his horse and _____ off into the sunset!
9 It's really exciting! We _____ for Paris tomorrow morning to start our holiday!

8 Pronunciation

/ɪ/ *sit* and /iː/ *see*

🔊 Turn to page 121.

9 Speak

(a) Work in pairs. Think of an interesting trip you have made.

Take it in turns to ask questions about your partner's trip. You have three minutes each. Make notes.

(b) Tell the story of your partner's trip. Your partner can make any changes or corrections. Then change roles.

(c) Tell your stories to another pair.

Round the world

10 Listen and read

a) 🔊 What exam results did the students get? Who did the best? Read, listen and check your answers.

Caroline: So what about a year off before we go to university? How does that grab you?

Joanne: Let's see what our results are like first.

Matt: Yeah, I'm kind of nervous. We might be studying for our exams again next year.

Ash: But if you did go away for a few months or so, where would you go?

Joanne: I really fancy going to South America.

Matt: Peru or Chile, that would be great.

Joanne: I fancy Brazil. All that sun and all those beaches.

Ash: And you could practise your Spanish too.

Joanne: In case you didn't know, Ash, they speak Portuguese in Brazil.

Caroline: I'd love to go somewhere in Asia. Somewhere on the other side of the world.

Joanne: What about India? It must be a fascinating place to visit.

Ash: I agree. I'd love to visit cities like Delhi and Bombay.

Joanne: It's called Mumbai these days, Ash.

Matt: Well, I want to go to Australia and do some real surfing.

Joanne: What about a bit of culture?

Matt: Oh, I'd spend a few days or so in Sydney, see the Opera House and stuff like that.

Caroline: And no, Ash. Before you say anything, Sydney's not the capital of Australia.

Ash: I know that. Perth is.

Caroline: Try Canberra, Ash.

Joanne: What about you, Ash? Where would you go?

Matt: Before Ash goes anywhere, he needs to get a map out and study the world a bit. Otherwise, he'd get lost!

Caroline: Look, there's Mr Crawford. And he's got the results with him.

Joanne: Come on then. Let's open them together. *A* in Physics, *B* in Chemistry and *B* in Maths. Not too bad. What about you, Caroline?

Caroline: *A* in Maths, *B* in English and *D* in History. They're OKish, I suppose.

Matt: No! Get out of here! I got an *E* in Geography. An *E*! That's a disaster!

Joanne: Take it easy, Matt! What about the others?

Matt: *A* in Economics and *A* in History.

Caroline: Two *A*s. That's not a disaster. That's brilliant.

Matt: Yeah, but an *E* in Geography!

Joanne: I'm so glad I didn't do Geography. It sounds like it was a bit of a nightmare.

Ash: I don't know about that.

Caroline: I'm sorry, Ash?

Ash: Well, I got two *A*s and a *B*.

Matt: What was the *B* in?

Ash: Geography! Who'd have believed it?

b) Answer the questions.

1 What does Matt think they might be doing next year and why?

2 Where does each of the students want to go and why?

3 What does Ash say that suggests he doesn't know very much about foreign countries?

4 How does each of them feel about their results?

11 Everyday English

(a) Find expressions 1–4 in the story. Who says them?

1 Take it easy!
2 How does that grab you?
3 a bit of a nightmare
4 Get out of here!

Which one means:

a It can't be true. ☐
b not a nice experience ☐
c Don't worry so much. ☐
d What do you think of that? ☐

(b) Complete the dialogues. Use the expressions in Exercise 11a.

1 A: I saw Mike with Jenny last night.
  B: ¹ .... ! They can't stand each other!

2 A: So, how did your date go last Saturday?
  B: Well, it was ² .... , to be honest! Just about everything went wrong!

3 A: Wow, I'm really, really hungry.
  B: OK, why don't we go to the Indian restaurant? ³ .... ?

4 A: I'm so angry about losing the match that I want to break something!
  B: ⁴ .... , Stuart! It isn't really that important, you know.

12 Write

(a) Read through the composition quickly. What is the writer's favourite place?

(b) Read the composition again.

1 What aspects of the room does the author focus on? What do these things tell us about the author?

2 The author asks two questions. What is the effect of these questions?

(c) To make your descriptive writing more interesting, make notes about the object you want to describe. Then experiment with different ways of combining this information until you reach the sentence you are most happy with.

Read the notes and combine the ideas to make sentences. Look back at the text and compare your sentences.

● tiny beach in Cornwall / family vacations / summer holidays – went on for ever
● grandparents' cottage in the country / garden with lots of flowers / birds singing all the time
● posters on wall / mostly pop-stars / change them every few months

(d) Choose three objects. Use this technique to write a couple of sentences about each one.

(e) Write about your favourite place in the whole world. Describe it and say why it is special to you.

My favourite place

There are many places that are special for me: a tiny beach in Cornwall where we used to spend family vacations during the endless summer holidays; my grandparents' country cottage with its garden full of wild flowers and birdsong; a photo in my geography textbook of a mountain scene in Switzerland, which I've only ever visited in my daydreams. All of these places have been special to me in their own way at various times in my life, but there is one place that has always been there for me, a place that I visit every day – my bedroom.

On the surface, my bedroom is pretty much like any other bedroom. It's got a door, a window and, of course, a bed. It's an unusual colour, though: bright red, like the red of a big, juicy tomato. I had a huge argument with my parents about the colour. They wanted me to paint it green because it would be good for my concentration. I told them red would be good for my imagination. I won and they even let me paint it myself. That was fun. Of course, another reason I love my bedroom is because it's where I keep all my things. I generally like to keep them all over the floor and under the bed – something else my parents and I occasionally disagree over.

What else can I tell you about my room? There are posters on the wall, usually of pop-stars, that tend to get changed every few months. There's a small table and chair beneath a window that overlooks the street below. Looking out of the window, I can spend hours watching the world go by while I pretend I'm working. And that's really all there is to say about it. So why do I like it so much? Well, because it's mine. It's a place I can escape to whenever I want. A place where I can be alone with my thoughts or share a joke with friends while we listen to music. It's the place where I do most of my thinking and have most of my ideas.

15 Movie magic

* Clauses of purpose: *to / in order to / so as to*
* Result clauses with *so / such (that)*
* Vocabulary: reacting to films

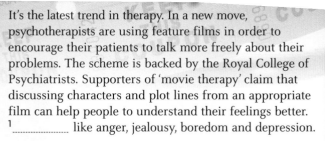

1 Read and listen

(a) Work in pairs. Discuss why you think people enjoy watching films so much.

(b) Read the text quickly and choose the best title.

1 Film stars have problems too
2 Films help unlock emotions
3 Watching films helps you relax

(c) 🔊 Put these phrases into the correct places in the text. Then listen and check.

a an example of the dangerous implications of not releasing anger
b he feels enormous betrayal
c films can bring to the surface the most deeply buried emotions
d claims he has used it successfully with about a third of his clients
e it allows them to confront psychological issues
f some distance from their immediate situation

(d) Read the text again and answer the questions.

1 Which organisation supports the use of films for therapy?
2 Which was the first film that Mr Wooder used for therapy?
3 With what percentage of clients has he been successful with film therapy?
4 Why is film therapy good with young people?
5 What did the film *Falling Down* help a client to understand?

Discussion box

Work in pairs or small groups. Discuss the questions together.

1 Do you go to the cinema often, and if so, does it help you feel good?
2 Do you think film therapy will be popular? Why / Why not?

It's the latest trend in therapy. In a new move, psychotherapists are using feature films in order to encourage their patients to talk more freely about their problems. The scheme is backed by the Royal College of Psychiatrists. Supporters of 'movie therapy' claim that discussing characters and plot lines from an appropriate film can help people to understand their feelings better. [1] _____ like anger, jealousy, boredom and depression.

One of those using the method is Bernie Wooder, a psychotherapist from Elstree, who charges £45 for a one-hour 'movie therapy' session. He said: 'I was counselling a woman who had been badly let down in a relationship, and who was experiencing such strong emotions that it was difficult for her to articulate them. I told her that her situation reminded me of *On the Waterfront*, when Marlon Brando's character realises his brother is corrupt and [2] _____ . My client identified so easily with him that she started to cry. Watching and discussing the film was a catalyst for unlocking all the feelings she had repressed. Each time she watched and cried, she felt better.'

Mr Wooder admits that film therapy does not work for everyone, but [3] _____ . It also works well with the young, who seem happier to relate to fictional characters than to real people. Films are something that offer them [4] _____ 'Freud said that images are the language of the unconscious and I believe films are too. Through their characters, plots and even music, [5] _____ .' He said that *Falling Down*, in which Michael Douglas portrays an unemployed man who is so frustrated that

he lashes out, was [6] _____ . 'I used this film with a client who was depressed because he held on to a lot of the anger he felt towards people who had frustrated him,' said Mr Wooder. The client watched the film and it had such an impact on him that he wanted to talk immediately. 'We talked about Michael Douglas's character and the disastrous path he takes, and my client then realised that he needed to let go of his emotions more regularly so as not to erupt like a time bomb. It was very therapeutic for him.'

2 Grammar

Clauses of purpose: *to / in order to / so as to*

(a) Look at the examples. Then complete the rule.

1 Discussing an appropriate film can help people <u>to understand</u> their feelings better.

2 Psychotherapists are using feature films <u>in order to encourage</u> their patients to talk about their problems.

3 He needed to let go of his emotions <u>so as not to erupt</u> like a time bomb.

Rule:

- We can use the *to* infinitive to talk about purpose. In more formal language, or in writing, we can use
  .... or ....
  + the verb.

- To make these expressions negative, we put *not* immediately before the word
  ....

(b) Match the questions with the answers. Then rewrite the question and answer as one sentence using the words in brackets.

1 Why do people go to therapists?
2 Why did she cry a lot?
3 Why did they go to the DVD store?
4 Why do people go to libraries?
5 Why do studios make films?
6 Why do psychiatrists' clients lie on a couch?

a get some films to watch. (to)
b borrow books. (to)
c make money. (so as to)
d get help with their problems. (in order to)
e relax. (so as to)
f release her emotions. (in order to)

1 *People go to therapists in order to get help with their problems.*

3 Grammar

Result clauses with *so / such (that)*

(a) Complete the sentences with the phrases in the box. Use the text to help you.

> such an impact   so frustrated   so easily
> such strong emotions

1 Michael Douglas portrays an unemployed man who is .... that he lashes out.

2 It had .... that the client wanted to talk immediately

3 She was experiencing .... that it was difficult for her to articulate them.

4 My client identified .... with him that she started to cry.

(b) Complete the rule. Write *so* or *such*.

Rule:

- In order to show how one thing is the result of another, we can use:
  .... + adjective/adverb +
  (*that*) ... or .... + *a* + noun /
  plural noun + (*that*) ...

(c) Join the two sentences to make one.

1 We were late. We had to take a taxi.
   We were so late that we had to take a taxi.
2 It was a moving film. I almost cried.
3 They were very bored by the film. They fell asleep.
4 He's a bad actor. You feel like laughing when you watch him.
5 Cinema tickets are expensive these days. More and more people hire DVDs.
6 Film therapy is effective. Many people overcome their problems.
7 Film therapy is an effective approach. It's backed by the Royal College of Psychiatrists.
8 Spielberg makes great films. He's known all over the world.

(d) Make sentences that are true for you, using the phrases in the box. Compare sentences with a partner.

> such a long time   such good friends   so tired
> so easily   so happy   such bad weather
> such a lot of homework   such a big mistake
> so often   so angry

I was so tired last weekend that I didn't do anything at all.
I had such a lot of homework that I couldn't go out.

Look

The word *that* can be left out, but we usually keep it in.

4 Pronunciation

Word stress in multi-syllabic words

🔊 Turn to page 121.

5 Speak

(a) Read the film descriptions. Have you seen any of the films? What kind of film do you think each one is? Choose from the types in the box.

> epic   horror   comedy   drama   thriller   romantic comedy

The Aviator

Leonardo diCaprio plays Howard Hughes, the famous millionaire who loved aeroplanes but ended up living as a recluse.

Alien 4

Sigourney Weaver is caught in a dilemma. This time, she finds the monster has been cloned from her body tissue. And this time, they're related – but how will she deal with that?

Cheaper by the Dozen

Steve Martin and his wife are trying to raise their family of twelve while balancing their careers at the same time.

Lost in Translation

Bill Murray feels alone and alienated in Tokyo as he looks around for ways to try and understand an unfamiliar lifestyle.

(b) Work with a partner. Read about these people with problems. They want to try film therapy. Which film would you recommend for each person? Explain why.

- Carl is a businessman and spends a lot of time away from home. His wife looks after their three young children, and she wants to have a career. Carl feels guilty that he's not around much to help.

- Pauline is 60. Her only son lives on the other side of the world in Australia. She hasn't seen him for five years and misses him terribly. She would love to see him but is terrified of flying.

- Sue had a daughter when she was only 18. She never truly accepted that she was a mother and this led to a lot of problems between her daughter and herself. Now her daughter's 16 and getting into trouble at school. Sue wants to help but she doesn't know how to.

- Claire has always lived in small towns. Recently she moved to a large city to start a new job. She has made very few friends and is finding it difficult to adapt to her new surroundings.

(c) What other films would you recommend to each of these people?

6 Listen

(a) 🔊 Listen to Vince and Cathy talking about the films of Steven Soderbergh and tick (✓) the boxes.

		Vince	Cathy
Who ...			
1	thought *Bubbles* was exciting?		
2	thought *Ocean's Twelve* was really funny?		
3	preferred *Ocean's Eleven* to *Ocean's Twelve*?		
4	thought *Erin Brockovich* was interesting?		
5	thought part of *Traffic* was sad?		
6	has seen *Fargo*?		

(b) 🔊 Listen again and answer the questions.

1 What do Cathy and Vince 'agree to differ' about?

2 Who was the actress in *Erin Brockovich*?

3 What is *Erin Brockovich* about?

4 Who almost dies in *Traffic*?

5 Why does Vince think *Fargo* is 'wonderful'?

7 Vocabulary

Reacting to films

a Read the quiz and fill in the spaces with the words in the box.

exciting   funny   sad   scary

What kind of film-goer are you? Do our film-goer's quiz and find out!

1 The hero gets up to make a wedding speech but he trips over and falls face first into the wedding cake.

a You *fall about laughing.* ☐
b You *chuckle* to yourself. ☐
c You can't understand what's so .... about the scene. ☐

2 The hero is slowly dying in his bed. In his arms he's holding his young son. With his final words he tells his son how much he loves him and asks him to look after the family.

a You *cry your eyes out.* ☐
b You're determined not to cry, so you *bite your lip.* ☐
c You can't understand what's so .... about the scene. ☐

3 The hero thinks he's being chased through a dark house by a monster. Suddenly the monster appears in front of him.

a You *scream* and *jump out of your seat.* ☐
b You don't see it because you've already closed your eyes. ☐
c You can't understand what's so .... about the scene. ☐

4 The hero is fighting lots of giant spiders when her gun runs out of bullets.

a You are *on the edge of your seat.* ☐
b You want to watch but you can't stop *yawning.* ☐
c You can't understand what's so .... about the film. ☐

b Do the quiz. Then check your scores on page 122.

c Look at the expressions in *italics*. Which means:

1 something you do when you are tired but trying not to fall asleep?
2 to laugh a lot?
3 to make a loud noise when you are scared?
4 to cry a lot?
5 to laugh quietly?
6 something you do when you are trying to stop yourself from crying?
7 you are very excited by a film?
8 something you might do when you are suddenly surprised?

d Complete the sentences with the expressions from Exercise 7a.

1 I was bored out of my brain, so I was .... all the time.
2 I didn't hear him come in, and I nearly .... seat.
3 It was so sad – I cried .... out.
4 I didn't want him to see me upset so I .... lip.
5 It was a great joke and we all .... laughing!
6 I was so nervous that I was on .... seat.

Culture in mind

8 Read

(a) Work with a partner. What do you know about Hollywood? Make notes.

(b) Read the texts quickly. What are the similarities/differences between Hollywood and Bollywood?

PLANET BOLLYWOOD

What is Bollywood?

Bollywood is the nickname given to the Indian film industry – it's a play on the word Hollywood. The B comes from Bombay (now known as Mumbai). Bollywood is massive. It makes up to 800 films a year – twice as many as Hollywood – and about 14 million Indian people go to the cinema every day. Films are made so quickly that sometimes actors on set shoot scenes for four different films at a time, using the same actors and the same backgrounds. And sometimes the scripts are even hand-written!

Where did it all start?

In 1899 the first Indian short film was screened, and Bollywood was born. Just like in Hollywood, the films were silent to begin with; then in the 1930s the films became 'talkies'. Many Indians came to live and work in Britain in the 1950s, and they brought their culture with them. Now, Bollywood's biggest audience outside India is in Britain.

Why is Bollywood so big now?

2002 was the year Bollywood took off in Britain. A season of Indian films was shown on TV when England played India in a big cricket tournament. A department store devoted a summer to Indian fashion, and shops everywhere were full of colourful Indian clothes, jewellery and henna. *Bombay Dreams*, a new West End musical, was a sell-out. Special cinemas also showed Bollywood classic films and had exhibitions featuring Bollywood film posters. *Lagaan*, a huge Bollywood hit, was nominated for an Oscar. The music charts were full of Bhangra music, with Timbaland, Dr Dre and the Neptunes

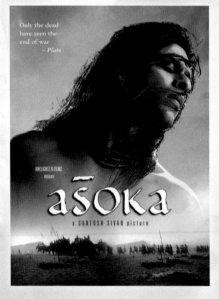

producing Indian beats, and Punjabi MC having big hits. India was even featured in cool car adverts. Now it's not only Indian families who watch the films made in Bollywood – they're shown in big cinemas across the country, while recent films like *Devdas, Veer-Zaara* and *Asoka* have been huge box-office successes in the UK.

What makes Bollywood films unusual?

Bollywood films are really colourful and full of singing, dancing and lots of costume changes. They also stick to a formula of: boy meets girl, they fall in love and they struggle for family approval. There's nearly always a love triangle with a hero, a heroine and another woman who's after the hero. Then there's a friend who's a bit of a comedy character. Romance is big, but there's no kissing on screen!

What problems does Bollywood face?

Bollywood's biggest problem is piracy – where people copy the films and either sell them or show them to other people for free. As a result, not all films produced make a profit, even though they can be seen by close to one billion people. If everyone paid to see films legally, the industry would make lots more money, and Bollywood film producers are working hard to try and find a way to prevent piracy.

Another problem is that younger generations are beginning to find the stories predictable and are bored with the similar story-lines. Film-makers are trying to solve this by changing plots to reflect the changes in modern Indian society – like the tendency of children in Indian families to go and study abroad, for example.

(c) Read the text again and answer the questions.

1 Where does the name Bollywood come from?
2 When did Indian films first come to Britain, and why?
3 What event in 2002 made Indian films more popular?
4 What is the plot of most Bollywood films?
5 What are Bollywood's two problems, and how are people trying to solve them?

9 Write

(a) Read through the synopsis of the film *School of Rock*.

1 Does the writer like the film?
2 What do you think Dewey's 'brilliant plan' might be?

(b) Read the synopsis again and answer the questions.

1 How much factual information is given about the film?
2 What tense is used to tell the story? Why do you think this tense is used?
3 How much of the story is told?
4 Why do you think the writer stops his synopsis where he does?

(c) Read the text again. What do the words in **bold** refer to? Why does the writer use them?

(d) Write a synopsis of a film you have seen recently. Think carefully about how you can use pronouns effectively to avoid repeating words.

Discussion box

Work in pairs or small groups. Discuss these questions together.

1 Do you know of other countries that have their own film industry?
2 What films are/were produced in your country?
3 What non-Hollywood films have you seen?

School of Rock is one of those rare films: a comedy for both teenagers and adults. **It** stars Jack Black as Dewey, a guitarist who won't give up **his** dream of living a rock 'n' roll lifestyle. But in the real world of overdue rent and his flatmate Ned's nagging girlfriend, **it**'s becoming almost impossible to achieve. However, Dewey has a plan – to win a $20,000 talent contest with **his** band. Unfortunately, the other band members decide that **his** on-stage clowning is embarrassing and that **they** have a better chance of winning without **him**. So one day Dewey arrives at rehearsal to find that the band has a new guitarist.

Things look bad for Dewey: no money and no band to win the competition. One day at home, Dewey answers a phone-call for Ned, **his** flatmate, who's a substitute teacher. A private school wants **his** services immediately. When Dewey learns that the job pays $600 a week, he pretends to be Ned. An hour later he is introducing himself to a room of ten year-olds as Mr S, **their** teacher for the next few weeks.

Of course, Dewey has no intention of teaching the kids anything. He puts **them** on permanent break time while he sits and daydreams. However, the next day, the children go for **their** weekly music lesson. While Dewey is in the toilet, he hears beautiful music outside. He goes and looks through the music room door. **There** he sees **his** kids playing a variety of instruments. And suddenly, Dewey has a brilliant plan to win that $20,000 after all.

16 Music in the air

* Indirect questions review
* Verbs + *wh-* clauses
* Vocabulary: making comparisons stronger
* Vocabulary: listening to music

1 Read and listen

(a) Make a list of places where you often hear music without choosing to.

(b) Read the article quickly. Which of these places does it mention?

(c) 🔊 Read the text again and add the sentences. Write a–e in the spaces. Then listen and check.

  a It has more than 27 million visitors spending over £770 million a year.

  b I just turn on the radio and listen to whatever comes on.

  c You don't want to play rock music and get them even more worked up.

  d But later on, it's quieter.

  e But if we've got a big cup match and we play *We Will Rock You*, they'll clap.

(d) Read the text again and answer the questions.

  1 When do they play relaxing music in the Bluewater Shopping Centre?

  2 Why is Liam Collins pretty sure that people actually listen to what they play in the shopping centre?

  3 How do they decide what music to play at Prenton Park football ground?

  4 What do taxi drivers have to do to keep their customers from complaining?

  5 Why do some people choose to play classical music?

A world of Music – but who chooses it?

Music is all around us – in shopping centres, at football grounds, in taxis, at the gym, and even in the dentist's waiting room. We can't get away from it, nor do we have any influence on what we have to listen to. However, we rarely think about who chooses the music, and we've no idea how they decide what to play.

'It's a science,' explains Liam Collins, 41, who is DJ at the Bluewater Shopping Centre in Kent. [1]_____ 'We don't play music in the shops themselves, but in the dining areas, entrance halls and the courtyards, you can hear a whole range of different music, from Paul Oakenfold mixes to the 1812 Overture and Frank Sinatra.'

Liam makes his selections by consulting music buyers at Virgin Megastores. 'In the morning, the music's generally on loud. [2]_____ . The busier the shopping centre gets, the more relaxing the music needs to be.' But I wonder whether the customers ever listen to the music. No one could be more certain about that than Liam. 'Once we accidentally played *White Christmas* at Easter. A huge crowd of people came to reception to tell us. People listen more carefully to the music than you might think.'

'I don't actually think the crowd care about the music, to be honest,' says Richie Tierney, PA announcer at Prenton Park football ground, the home of Tranmere Rovers. '[3]_____ .' Otherwise Richie and his assistant have clear rules. They play James Brown's *I Feel Good* when Tranmere score, and they play a special re-mix of *Going Home* by Mark Knopfler when people are leaving the stadium.

We also spoke to several taxi drivers. What is important for them is to have music playing, but what they actually listen to is nothing like as important as how loudly they play it. 'We play everything from Coldplay to the Spice Girls, Robbie Williams and Alicia Keys. No one complains about what it is, but the minute it gets too loud, then people complain.' 'I don't really care what I listen to,' says Jed Strange, a London cabby. '[4]_____ But I do change the music if the customer doesn't like it. That way, the tips I get are much better,' he admits. We also found a taxi driver who only plays classical music. 'Classical music is just as enjoyable as rock,' he says. 'With classical music I feel far more relaxed, and I really need that with today's traffic, which is getting a lot worse every day.'

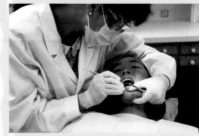

And in that he's not alone – classical music is also the preferred choice of Dr Janet Highsmith, a dentist from Cambridge. 'Most of my patients are pretty stressed,' she says. '[5]_____ . It's usually a piece of Baroque music that helps them to relax.'

Discussion box

Work in pairs or small groups.
Discuss these questions together.

1 For each of the places in the text, say which kind of music you think is most suitable and why.

2 What kind of influence does music have on you in various situations? In what way, for example, does it influence your behaviour as a customer in a shop?

2 Grammar

Indirect questions (1)

a Read the sentences. Then complete the direct questions below.

*We've no idea **how they decide**.*

*I wonder **whether the customers ever listen to the music**.*

1 How .... decide?
2 Do .... ever listen to the music?

b Complete the rule. Write *never, invert, don't invert, sometimes*.

Rule:

- When we use *wh-* question words in direct questions we usually .... the subject and the verb, and we .... use *do / does / did*.
- We can also use *wh-* question words in statements (indirect questions). In indirect questions we .... the word order and we .... use *do / does / did*.

c Join the two sentences to make one.

1 Where did everyone go? I wonder.
   I wonder where everyone went.
2 How much does it cost? I don't know.
3 Where do people buy CDs? It's easy to find out.
4 When do people need to listen to music to relax? We don't always know.
5 How often do they change the music they play in shops? I'm not sure.
6 When was music first played in shops? I wonder.

3 Vocabulary

Making comparisons stronger

a Complete the table with the words in the box. Then check in the text on page 108.

more   worse   as   nothing like   far   lot

1 Classical music is	*just*	.... enjoyable as rock.
2 Rock music gets patients	*even*	.... worked up.
3 That way, the tips I get are	*much*	better.
4 The traffic in London is getting	*a*	.... every day.
5 What they listen to is	....	as important.
	not nearly	
6 With classical music I feel	....	more relaxed.

b Which of the sentences in the table:

1 are making a comparison?
2 emphasises similarity, not difference?

c Make these comparisons stronger. There is often more than one possibility. Try to use a different phrase from Exercise 3a each time.

1 Shopping centres would be nicer without music.
2 MP3 players are cheaper than they used to be.
3 Classical music is more relaxing to listen to than dance music.
4 The piano is harder to learn than the guitar.
5 CDs should be less expensive than they are.
6 Films are as enjoyable as music.
7 Learning English isn't as difficult as some people think.
8 Music isn't as important as many people say it is.

d Which of the sentences in Exercise 3c do you agree with?

4 Speak

Complete the sentences for yourself. Then compare sentences in pairs.

1 No music is more relaxing for me than …
2 I pay far more attention to music when … than …
3 I think it would be a lot better to play … in/at
4 … is much less important to me than …
5 … is nothing like as enjoyable for me as …
6 … is much worse than …

5 Listen

a Look at the photographs. Do you recognise the instruments? Which of them have you heard?

b Match the instruments with the countries.

1	berimbau	a	Australia
2	bagpipes	b	Trinidad
3	didgeridoo	c	Indonesia
4	bonang	d	Switzerland
5	alphorn	e	Brazil
6	steel drum	f	Scotland

c 🔊 Listen to a music expert talking about the instruments. Check your answers to Exercise 5b.

d 🔊 Listen again and answer the questions.

1 Where, apart from the British Isles, are bagpipes played?

2 What were alphorns used for, and on what occasions are they played today?

3 In what kind of ceremonies were didgeridoos played?

4 How many types of steel drum are there?

5 How many steel drum players are there usually in a band?

6 How many strings does the berimbau have and where did it come from originally?

7 What instrument is used to play gamelan music?

e 🔊 Listen again to the instruments. Can you name them? Which one do you like most / least?

6 Vocabulary

Listening to music

a Read the sentences about music. Match the underlined words to the definitions.

1 'I prefer songs to instrumental music.'

2 'I love being in the car and singing along to the songs on the radio.'

3 'I'm a hopeless singer, so I usually just whistle or hum along!'

4 'I don't really enjoy recorded music on the radio or on CDs. I prefer live music.'

5 'I'm not really interested in the lyrics – it's the tune that's important for me.'

6 'Dance music's my favourite – it's got a great beat.'

7 'Sometimes I hear a song and then I can't get it out of my head!'

8 'I really hate the muzak you hear in supermarkets and shopping malls.'

a the words

b stop thinking about it

c make a musical noise with your lips together

d music composed for instruments, not voices

e music played in front of an audience

f music played in a studio and put on a CD or tape

g melody

h sing as you listen

i music played in shops or restaurants to increase sales

j musical pulse or rhythm

b) Which of the sentences in Exercise 6a (if any) are true for you? Change them to make them true for you.

I prefer instrumental music to songs.

c) Work with a partner. Compare your ideas.

7 Pronunciation

record (noun) vs. re*cord* (verb) (etc.)

🔊 Turn to page 121.

8 Grammar

Indirect questions (2)

a) Here are three questions that the interviewer asked. (Circle) the correct options.

1 Can I ask you where *you went?* / *did you go?*

2 Can you tell us where *it's from* / *is it from?*

3 Do we know when *they were first developed* / *were they first developed?*

b) Underline the *wh-* question words in the questions.

c) (Circle) the correct option to complete the rule.

> **Rule:**
>
> • When we want to be polite we often use the following phrases to ask people for information: *Can you tell me ...? Can I ask you ...? Could you tell me ...? Do you know ...?* This is sometimes followed by a *wh-* question word, in which case the word order is the same as in a *statement* / *question*.

d) Read the interview. Rewrite the questions using the words in brackets.

A: What's your favourite music? (**Can you tell me**)
¹Can you tell me what your favourite music is?

B: Yes, it's disco music.

A: When did disco music start? (**Do you know**)
² _____

B: Oh, back in the 1970s, I think!

A: I see. How many disco CDs have you got? (**Do you know exactly**) ³ _____

B: Oh, hundreds – I've lost count of them!

A: Where do you keep them? (**Could you tell us**)
⁴ _____

B: Yeah, on the shelves in my room.

A: How much money have you spent on them? (**Have you got any idea**) ⁵ _____

B: Oh, I've lost count of that too. I don't want to think about it!

A: Which was the first disco record you bought? (**Can you remember**) ⁶ _____

B: No, sorry, I can't remember.

A: Which piece of disco music do you like the most? (**Can you tell me**) ⁷ _____

B: I guess it's *Lost in Music* by Sister Sledge.

A: How often do you listen to it? (**Can you tell me**)
⁸ _____

B: Oh, not very often – but sometimes I put it on in my car! It's still brilliant!

e) Work with a partner. Ask and answer the questions from Exercise 8d.

9 Speak

Work in pairs or small groups. Discuss the questions.

> classical rock hip-hop dance country folk pop disco

I didn't like [XXX] a few years ago, but now _____

When I was younger, I hated classical music. But now I like it a lot more than before.

1 Which of these kinds of music do you like/dislike?

2 Have you always liked them or has your opinion about them changed?

3 Which is your favourite song / piece of music / singer / band?

10 Speak and listen

a Match phrases 1–5 with definitions a–e. Then find the phrases in the song.

1 my 9 to 5
2 first to go
3 my salvation
4 in the spotlight
5 plays so very tight

a plays music in a very professional and precise way
b the thing that saves me (for example, from boredom)
c the focus of attention
d my regular daytime job
e the first thing that someone loses

b Listen to the song and fill in the spaces.

Lost in Music
by Sister Sledge

(chorus)

We're lost in music, caught in a ¹_____ ,
No turning back, we're lost in music

We're lost in music, feel so ²_____ ,
I quit my 9 to 5, we're lost in music.

Have you ever seen some people lose everything?
First to go is their mind.
Responsibility to me is a ³_____ ,
I'll get a job some other time.

I want to join a band, and play in front of crazy ⁴_____
Yes, I call that temptation.
Give me the melody, that's all that I ever need,
The music is my salvation.

(chorus)

Mmm, hmm, in the spotlight, the ⁵_____ plays so very tight,
Each and every night.
It's not vanity, to me it's my sanity,
I could never ⁶_____

Some people ask me 'What are you gonna be?
Why don't you go get a job?'
All that I could say, I won't give up my music,
Not me, not now, no way, no how, oh...oh...

(chorus)

Did you know ...?

Sister Sledge were formed in 1971 in North Philadelphia and were first called Sisters Sledge. The four sisters (Kim, Debbie, Joni and Kathy Sledge) were aged between 12 and 16 years old when they started singing. Debbie, the eldest, was the first to join a singing group, and she taught harmony to her sisters. Their biggest success came in 1979 with the disco hit *We are Family*, which still fills the dance floor today.

11 Write

(a) Read the descriptions of different types of writing and match them with examples A–C.

1 **Mini-sagas**
A mini-saga is a story of <u>exactly</u> fifty words. Like all good stories it must have a beginning, a middle and an end.

2 **Limericks**
A limerick is a humorous five-line poem with a special rhythm and rhyming scheme.

3 **Haiku**
Haiku is a traditional type of Japanese poetry. The poems are about everyday things and are usually three short lines which don't rhyme.

A
Curving up, then down.
Meeting blue sky and green earth
Mixing sun and rain.

B
She was crying as she took the skin off. This had happened many times before. It was agony every time she did it. She dried her eyes and put down the knife. This must be the last time – but on the other hand, her husband loved onions in his soup.

C
There was an old lady from Crewe,
Who dreamed she was eating her shoe.
She woke in the night
And got quite a fright –
She found it was perfectly true.

(b) Which one do you like best? Why? Discuss your choice with your partner.

(c) Choose one or two of these writing types and try writing your own. Here are some tips to help you.

Mini-sagas
- think of a story (one you already know, or invent one). It shouldn't be very complicated, but it should have a beginning, a middle and an end.
- write a first draft – remember, in the end you want <u>exactly</u> 50 words!
- count the number of words in your first draft. If you have too many words, cut out adjectives; replace nouns with pronouns; use participle clauses instead of full verb forms (*Walking down the street, he saw ...' is shorter than 'He walked down the street and then he saw ...'*) If you have too few words, add some adjectives; add words like *then, next, suddenly, a few minutes later*.

Limericks
- the lines must rhyme in this sequence: AABBA
- lines 1, 2 and 5 have seven to ten syllables and rhyme with one another, lines 3 and 4 have five to seven syllables and also rhyme with each other.
- remember there is a strong rhythm, like this:
  da DUM da da DUM da da DUM
  da DUM da da DUM da da DUM
  da DUM da da DUM
  da DUM da da DUM
  da DUM da da DUM da da DUM
- limericks usually begin with *There was a ... from ...* , but they don't have to!
- they should have a joke in the last line.

Haiku
- choose a topic, for example *rain, traffic, old people, mountains*.
- write three short lines. The first line usually contains five syllables, the second line seven syllables, and the third line five syllables. Very often, a haiku does not have any complete verb forms. Look at example A – only *-ing* forms are used.

(d) Swap texts with your classmates. Have fun!

Module 4 **Check your progress**

1 **Grammar**

a) Complete the sentences using the correct form of the verb in brackets.

1 He __is believed__ (believe) to be in the United States.
2 Many children _____ (think) to be extremely talented.
3 People in tribes in the Vaupes river region _____ (know) to speak several languages.
4 English _____ (think) to have one of the biggest vocabularies of any language.
5 German _____ (say) to have more irregular verbs than regular ones.
6 More languages _____ (expect) to die out during the next fifty years.
7 Many languages_____ (think) to come from Sanskrit centuries ago.

| | 6 |

b) Put the sentences together and write one sentence.

1 He smiled to himself. He wrote the letter.
   Smiling to himself, he wrote the letter.
2 He wrote the letter. Then he posted it.
   Having written the letter, he posted it.
3 She looked out of the window. She thought about her father.

4 She walked through the valley. She felt at one with nature.

5 They climbed the mountain. Then they sat down to look at the view.

6 He swam across the lake. Then he collapsed on the shore.

7 We saw the *aurora borealis*. We gasped in amazement.

8 They saw the waterfall ahead of them. Then they tried to change direction.

| | 6 |

c) Write sentences with *didn't need to* or *needn't have*.

1 We took raincoats but they weren't necessary.
   We needn't have taken raincoats.
2 It wasn't raining so we didn't take our raincoats.

3 I studied all weekend, but the test on Monday was cancelled.
4 There was no test so I didn't study at the weekend.

5 We didn't cook any food because there was a restaurant.
6 I bought him some chocolate, but he told me he is allergic to it.

| | 5 |

d) Combine the sentences into one. Use the words in brackets.

1 They went to London. They wanted to do some shopping. (in order)
   They went to London in order to do some shopping.
2 I studied hard. I wanted to get better marks than last time. (so as)

3 He wore his best clothes. He wanted to impress her. (in order)

4 She put the money in her pocket. She didn't want to lose it. (in order)

5 We kept very quiet. We didn't want to disturb him. (so as)

| | 4 |

e) Circle the correct word in each sentence.

1 He was *so* / *such* / *such a* tired that he fell asleep immediately.
2 It was *so* / *such* / *such a* delicious food that I couldn't stop eating.
3 The test was *so* / *such* / *such a* easy that I left 30 minutes before the end.
4 They're *so* / *such* / *such a* good friends that I can't imagine being without them.
5 My brother was *so* / *such* / *such a* angry that I thought he was going to hit me!
6 My sister is *so* / *such* / *such a* good writer that they're going to publish her book.

| | 5 |

(f) Rewrite the sentences/questions.

1 What's his name? I don't know.
   I don't know what his name is.

2 How many people were there at the party? Do you know?

   ....

3 What time do the shops open? I have no idea.

   ....

4 When does the concert start? Let's find out.

   ....

5 What did they want to know? Can you tell me?

   ....

6 Who did the teacher say was responsible? I don't know.

   ....

   [ ] 5

2 Vocabulary

(a) Complete each sentence using a word from the box.

> word ~~make out~~ gist catch lost pick

1 He spoke so quietly that I couldn't _make out_ what he was saying.

2 I'm sorry, but I didn't understand a .... of what you just said.

3 My Spanish is very poor, so he .... me completely after two sentences.

4 Could you repeat that, please? I didn't quite .... it.

5 I got the .... of the lecture.

6 Don't try to understand everything – just see if you can .... out the important words.

   [ ] 5

(b) Unscramble the letters to make a word that completes the sentences.

1 I was so surprised that I _jumped_ (jupedm) out of my seat.

2 It was very exciting – I was on the .... (gede) of my seat.

3 It was an incredibly funny joke and everyone .... (lefl) about laughing.

4 The film was so sad that I .... (riecd) my eyes out.

5 I wanted to argue with him, but I decided to .... (tibe) my lip and say nothing.

6 The comedy was quite funny and I .... (cklucehd) quietly to myself.

   [ ] 5

(c) Write the correct word in each space to complete the puzzle.

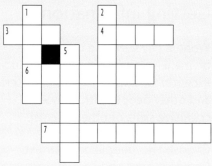

Across

3 A part of the coastline where the sea is surrounded by land on three sides

4 A large area of fresh water surrounded by land

6 A very large piece of ice that moves down a valley

7 A rock like ridge made up of tiny skeletons of marine animals under the surface of the sea

Down

1 The Andes is a mountain .... in South America

2 A large flat area of land

5 A narrow valley with steep sides   7

(d) Mark the sentences T (true) or F (false). Correct the false statements.

1 Instrumental music is music that doesn't have singing. _T_

2 When you whistle or hum along to a song, you sing the words.

3 Another way of describing music with a good rhythm is to say it's got a good beat.

4 When you can't get a song out of your head, you can't stop singing it.

5 The words of a song are called the tune.

    4

How did you do?

Tick (✓) a box for each section.

Total score:	☺	☻	☹
52	Very good	OK	Not very good
Grammar	24 – 31	16 – 23	less than 16
Vocabulary	16 – 21	11 – 15	less than 11

Project 1

A class presentation: a unique mind

1 Getting information

(a) Work in pairs. Make a list of some of 'mankind's greatest minds' (include exceptional artists, inventors, writers, and other people with unique cognitive skills or other talents).

(b) Choose two people on your list. Compare your choices with other pairs. Make sure you've chosen different people.

(c) Working on your own, do some research on the two people you have selected. Make notes on the key points. These could include key biographical details (where/when they were born), key events in their lives or important things they said.

(d) Compare notes with your partner. Decide which of the two people you want to use for your presentation. (Which one do you have the most interesting information about?) Now do some more detailed research. Here are some ideas:

- What is unique about the person?
- What can you find out about the person's thinking?
- What interesting quotations by the person can you find?
- What can you find out about the person's life, their social status, what they have achieved, and what other people have thought and said about them?
- What stories or anecdotes can you find about them?
- What is most interesting about them for you personally?

2 Prepare the presentation

(a) Create a mind map of the main points you want to cover in your presentation.

(b) You will do your presentation in pairs. With your partner, decide who is going to talk about each point. Make sure you both have interesting content to talk about.

(c) In pairs, rehearse the presentation. Give each other feedback. Use these questions to help you.

What did you like most about your partner's presentation?
How could it be improved?
Are there any suggestions on language you would like to make?
Any other suggestions/observations?

Give each other feedback in a helpful way. Use phrases like:

What I really liked about your presentation was ...
You could also include ...
You said... Maybe you could ...
I found it difficult to understand what you said about ...
Do you think you could give a concrete example about ...?

3 The presentation

(a) Each pair takes turns to give their presentation to the rest of the class. Meanwhile, your classmates write down questions they would like to ask the person you are talking about.

(b) Your classmates ask their questions. You and your partner take turns answering the questions, as if you were the person you gave your presentation about. If you don't know the answer to a question, make it up as best as you can, based on what you have learnt about the person.

For your portfolio

Project 2

A group presentation: design your own charity

1 Do your research

(a) Work in groups of four. You are going to invent and organise a charity. First decide on who or what your charity will help. Brainstorm ideas. These could include people, animals or the environment. Decide whether your charity will work locally or nationally.

(b) When you have agreed on your area, think about what your charity's aims will be. What sort of help will you offer? How will you raise funds? How will your charity make a difference? Make a list of your aims.

(c) Think of a name for the charity. You also need to think of a slogan (a short phrase that people will remember and that describes quickly, in up to ten words, what your charity does) and a logo (a design).

(d) Discuss how your charity will work. Think about the following:

- How will you get other people to help you?
- Will you ask for money or for volunteers, or both?
- How will you raise money? What sort of fundraising events will you organise?
- What will you do with the money? Will you use it to buy equipment for the charity or give to the people you want to help?

2 Prepare the presentation

(a) Design a poster to advertise your charity. Your poster should clearly show your charity's name, its logo and slogan. Then it should show in some way, through both words and pictures, who you're going to help and what you're going to do. If you have time, you could also make small leaflets to hand out to people telling them about your charity.

(b) Prepare your presentation. Decide who is going to talk on each aspect of the charity. Make short notes on small cards of the key points you are going to talk about. In your groups, rehearse the presentation, giving each other feedback. Use the phrases from Project 1 to help you. Remember to look up when you are speaking.

3 The presentation

(a) Groups take turns to give their presentation to the rest of the class.

(b) Now it's time to put your charity idea into action! Good luck!

For your portfolio

Project 3
A class survey: your ecological footprint

For your portfolio

1 Choose the area you want to research

(a) You are going to carry out a survey to find out the size of your class's ecological footprint. As a class, make a list of topics you could ask questions about. These could include:

- travel
- holidays
- food and shopping
- energy use and recycling

(b) In groups of three or four, think about what sort of questions will help you decide on the class's ecological footprint. Brainstorm each topic for five minutes. Think about:

- what types of shop your classmates go to
- how much packaging there is on the food they eat
- where the food comes from (is it grown locally?) and whether it is organic
- what types of holiday people go on
- whether they help the local economy or whether they stay in big international hotels
- whether they leave the environment clean and tidy

Choose one person to make notes.

2 Prepare and carry out the survey

(a) Using your notes, write questions for your questionnaire. Think about what type of questions you are going to ask, and what the scoring scheme will be. Decide whether a high score will mean a big ecological footprint or a small one. Use the example questions to help you:

> **Yes/No questions**
> Do you think about where something was made before you buy it?
>
> **Ranking**
> How often do you walk, cycle or get the bus?
> Circle: never / once or twice a week / every day
>
> **Open questions**
> What should be done to help keep energy use as low as possible at home?

Remember that you are trying to work out the size of your class's ecological footprint, so you will need to design questions that tell you this clearly.

(b) Use your questionnaire. Decide which members of the class each of you is going to interview. Carry out the interviews and note down your classmates' answers.

3 Write up the results

(a) Collate your results and work out a total score. Does your class have a big or a small ecological footprint?

(b) Write a report on the results. You can draw charts or graphs to illustrate some of the results.

How do you get to school?

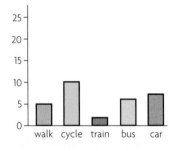

4 Present your report

Present your report to the class. Discuss your results with the rest of the class. Do you all agree on the size of your class's footprint? How can you make the footprint smaller?

Project 4
An information booklet: a foreign country

1 The task

You are going to make a booklet about a country (not your own) that you think is interesting. Include information about:

- the country's geography and climate

  are there any mountains / lakes / rivers / places of particular interest?

  what kind of weather does the country have at different times of the year?

- the people who live there

  are there many different ethnic groups?

  what is/are the main religion(s)?

  what is/are the language(s) of the country?

  what kind of clothes do people wear?

- some aspects of the culture

  history (one or two important moments)

  politics (is it a democracy? a republic? a kingdom?)

  music, dance, literature, art

2 Do your research

(a) Work with a partner. Choose a country (one that you think your classmates will be interested in, and perhaps don't know very much about).

(b) Research the information and make notes. You could use:

- the internet
- the library in your school
- people you know who come from the country

3 Design your booklet

(a) Find pictures for your booklet (from the internet, magazines) or (if you want to) draw some pictures. Include a map of the country.

(b) Write an introductory paragraph saying why you chose this country.

(c) Organise the information you have found into sections (like those outlined above in Part 1), and think of a heading for each section. Choose the most interesting facts to include.

(d) Write up your notes into paragraphs, and add illustrations wherever you can.

(e) Write a contents page.

4 Presentation

Do a presentation on your country for the rest of the class. Be prepared to answer questions.

For your portfolio

Pronunciation exercises

Unit 1

/ð/ _the_ and /θ/ _thing_

a 🔊 Listen and put the words into the correct columns.

thing   the   three   these   that
them   this   think   thanks
therefore   thirty   thief

ð	θ
the	thing

b 🔊 Listen and repeat.

1   Therefore, I think it's over there.
2   This is just the thing I need!
3   Put them over there with that one.
4   I'd like these three things, thanks.
5   The theme of his theory was very thoughtful.
6   I think that the thief was thirty.

Unit 2

Consonant clusters

a 🔊 Listen and pay attention to how the underlined parts of the words are pronounced.

1   He's a general practitioner.
2   What's the diagnosis?
3   He appears to be completely healthy.
4   People think placebos are worthless.
5   The doctor gave me a prescription.
6   Some medicines are extracts from herbs and plants.

b 🔊 Listen again and repeat.

Unit 3

Intonation in questions

a 🔊 Listen to the questions. Does the speaker's voice go up ↑ or down ↓ at the end. Write ↑ (up) or ↓ (down).

1   Where are you going for your holiday this year?
2   Are you going somewhere nice?
3   Have you got any plans for the weekend?
4   When did you go to Rome?
5   Did you enjoy your holiday?
6   What did you see there?
7   Who went with you?

b Can you make a 'rule' about intonation in questions?

c 🔊 Listen again and repeat.

Unit 4

Schwa /ə/ _teacher_

a 🔊 Listen and notice how the underlined words are pronounced (shortened).

1   We need to finish but we're running out of time!
2   You should take some time off and go for a holiday.
3   I spent a lot of time talking to my friends on the phone.
4   I was just too late to see the thing I wanted to watch.
5   Look at the clock – we're not at all late for the lesson.
6   We spent more than a bit of time on a bus to go home.

b 🔊 Listen again and repeat.

Unit 5

Sentence stress and rhythm

a 🔊 Listen to the sentences. Notice the stress, and the rhythm of the sentences.

1   What I like about her is that she says 'thank you'.
2   What makes him seem rude is that he never smiles.
3   What really annoys me is that he just doesn't listen.
4   I always forget what I should do in formal situations.
5   I don't remember what it was that she told me.
6   It's important to know what people expect from us.

b 🔊 Listen again and repeat.

Unit 6

/æ/ _apple_ and /e/ _lemon_

a 🔊 Listen and tick (✓) the word you hear.

1   sat / set
2   pat / pet
3   bat / bet
4   tan / ten
5   pan / pen
6   band / bend
7   man / men
8   sad / said

b 🔊 Listen and repeat.

1   The men in the band sat down.
2   What the man said was sad.
3   If the pen bends, it's bad.
4   I bet ten pounds it isn't a real tan.

Unit 7

Linking sounds (intrusive /w/ and /j/)

a 🔊 Listen to the sentences. Pay attention to the underlined sounds. Next to each one write y (if you hear a /j/ sound) or w (if you hear a /w/).

1   That's for me and the next nine people.
2   I didn't know how to do it properly.
3   I've bought you a coffee.
4   Another cup of coffee or tea.
5   In London it is too easy to keep your head down.
6   It's a club whose members carry out good deeds.

b 🔊 Listen again and repeat.

Unit 8

Linking sounds

a 🔊 Listen and notice how the underlined sounds are pronounced.

1   I don't want to argue any more – let's make up!
2   It isn't always a good idea to make deals.
3   I'm sure we can sort out an answer.
4   Let's sit down and sort something out.
5   Let's try to find a solution.
6   I've tried hard but I can't find the answer!
7   I always get stuck with these maths problems.
8   Perhaps we should get a friend to help us!

b 🔊 Listen again and repeat.

Unit 9
Contractions in 3rd conditionals

a 🔊 Listen to these sentences. How are the <u>underlined</u> words pronounced?

1 If <u>I had</u> decided to get married at 16, my decision <u>would have</u> affected my wife and me.
2 If <u>I had</u> been given the vote at 16, my choice <u>could have</u> affected many more people.

b 🔊 Listen and repeat. Pay attention to the contractions.

1 If <u>she'd</u> asked me, I <u>would've</u> told her.
2 I <u>would've</u> bought it for you if <u>I'd</u> had enough money.
3 If <u>we'd</u> left any later, we <u>would've</u> missed the train.
4 We <u>would've</u> won the game if <u>he'd</u> scored that penalty.
5 If <u>you'd</u> have been nicer to him, he <u>might've</u> said 'yes'.

Unit 10
Contracted forms of *will have*

a 🔊 Listen to these sentences and notice how the <u>underlined</u> sounds are pronounced.

1 <u>I'll have</u> finished by five.
2 Don't worry. <u>He'll have</u> forgotten by tomorrow.
3 Slow down. <u>You'll have</u> finished before I've even started.
4 It was a secret! <u>She'll have</u> told everyone by tomorrow morning.
5 <u>We'll have</u> done all our exams by next Monday.
6 <u>They'll have</u> been married 25 years in July.

b 🔊 Listen again and repeat.

Unit 11
Intonation in question tags

a 🔊 Listen to the sentences. Does the speaker's voice go up or down at the end? Write ↑ (up) or ↓ (down).

1 It could be interesting, couldn't it?
2 You don't live around here, do you?

3 It wasn't a problem for you, was it?
4 She's French, isn't she?
5 They didn't tell you anything, did they?
6 You should try harder, shouldn't you?
7 You would help me, wouldn't you?

b 🔊 In which of the sentences is the speaker a) looking to check information? b) just making conversation? Listen again and repeat.

c Practise saying the sentences in Exercise a. Say each one:
i as if you were looking to check information.
ii as if you were just making conversation.

Unit 12
Shifting stress

a 🔊 Listen to this sentence said in different ways. Each time <u>underline</u> the word that has the greatest stress.

1 Roughly half the population speak English as a second language.
2 Roughly half the population speak English as a second language.
3 Roughly half the population speak English as a second language.

b Which of the sentences above might well be followed with:
1 not French.
2 not three quarters.
3 not as a first language.

c Practise saying the sentence, changing the stress for meanings a, b and c.

It takes me more or less ten minutes to get to school.
a not 20 minutes
b not my brother
c not the bus station

Unit 13
Words ending in *-ough*

a 🔊 Listen and repeat.
1 cough
2 enough
3 through
4 though
5 tough
6 thorough

b 🔊 Listen and repeat.
1 He coughed all through the night.
2 They weren't tough enough.
3 We need to be very thorough, though.

Unit 14
/ɪ/ *sit* and /iː/ *see*

a 🔊 Listen and tick (✓) the word you hear.
1 beat / bit
2 seat / sit
3 feet / fit
4 green / grin
5 heat / hit
6 neat / knit
7 sheep / ship
8 wean / win

b 🔊 Listen and repeat.
1 Don't sit on your feet.
2 You win – you beat me!
3 We need a bit of heat in here.
4 If you hit three sheep, you win!

Unit 15
Word stress in multi-syllabic words

a 🔊 Listen and mark the stress on each word.
1 therapy
2 therapeutic
3 medicine
4 medicinal
5 comedy
6 comedian
7 identify
8 identification

b 🔊 Listen and repeat the words.

Unit 16
record (noun) vs. re*cord* (verb) (etc.)

a 🔊 Listen and mark the stress on the words in *italics*.
1 The band made a *record*.
2 They *recorded* the song in Ireland.
3 The gold was *extracted* from a mine in Colombia.
4 Did you like the *extract* we read in the last unit?
5 She signed a *contract* with a record company.
6 They *contracted* her to make two CDs.
7 Science has *progressed* through the centuries.
8 We've made a lot of *progress*.

b 🔊 Listen again and repeat.

Speaking exercises: extra material

Unit 4, page 25, Exercise 5

Student B: Ask your partner these questions and answer their questions. Student A starts.

> 1 Do you sometimes take time to 'do nothing'?
>
> 2 How do you react when you are writing a test and you notice that you are running out of time?
>
> 3 How much time do you spend shopping every week?
>
> 4 Do you ever feel that you spend too much time on things? If so, what?

Unit 5, page 34, Exercise 1

How confident are you?

1: a = 1 b = 3 c = 2   4: a = 3 b = 2 c = 1
2: a = 2 b = 3 c = 1   5: a = 2 b = 1 c = 3
3: a = 3 b = 2 c = 1

1–6 points You are extremely worried about how other people see you and always want to make a good impression. You are afraid of looking silly or weak. What you need to realise is that no-one ever comes across as being perfect all the time. Try to relax a bit more. It's only human to make mistakes sometimes.

8–12 points Maybe you can try to be a little less self-conscious. Many psychologists agree that other people tend to judge us more kindly than we judge ourselves. So don't worry too much about getting into embarrassing situations. In five minutes no-one will remember what happened anyway.

13–15 points You're not exactly shy, are you? And you don't mind if you seem a bit ridiculous at times. This is what makes you come across as very confident. And you're absolutely right – it's good not to take life too seriously!

Think of another situation for the questionnaire. Write it down with three multiple-choice answers. Ask your partner to read it and choose their answer. Then discuss in pairs.

Unit 10, page 71, Exercise 8

Student B: Circle the correct time expressions. Then ask your partner the questions. Student A starts.

> 1 How long have you got *until / by* you finish school?
>
> 2 What changes do you think you'll see in your life *during / for* the next five years?
>
> 3 What will you be doing six hours *from / in* now?

Unit 15, page 105, Exercise 7

Mostly A answers: You're a film-maker's dream! Whatever reaction they want from you, they get it!

Mostly B answers: Perhaps you need to lighten up a little at the movies?

Mostly C answers: Why do you go to the cinema at all? It's obvious that you're just not into films!

✳ Wordlist

(v) = verb　　(n) = noun　　(adj) = adjective　　(adv) = adverb

Unit 1

Autism

ability (n) /ə'bɪlətɪ/
Asperger's syndrome (n)
　/'æs,pɜːɡəs ,sɪndrəʊm/
autistic (adj) /ɔː'tɪstɪk/
developmental (adj)
　/dɪ,veləp'mentəl/
diagnose (v) /'daɪəɡnəʊz/
disorder (n) /di'sɔːdə/
drawing (n) /'drɔːɪŋ/
imaginary (adj) /ɪ'mædʒɪnərɪ/
memorise (v) /'meməraɪz/
mute (adj) /mjuːt/
relationship (n) /rɪ'leɪʃənʃɪp/
talent (n) /'tælənt/

Expressions with *mind*

be in two minds (v) /biː ɪn tuː
　'maɪndz/
be out of (your) mind (v) /biː
　aʊt əv jə maɪnd/
change (your) mind (v)
　/tʃeɪnd' jə maɪnd/
have got something on (your)
　mind (v) /hæv ɡɒt
　'sʌmθɪŋ ɒn jə maɪnd/
keep (something) in mind (v)
　/kiːp 'sʌmθɪŋ ɪn maɪnd/
make up (your) mind (v) /meɪk
　ʌp jə maɪnd/
read (someone's) mind (v) /riːd
　sʌmwnz 'maɪnd/
slip (your) mind (v) /slɪp jə
　'maɪnd/
speak (your) mind (v) /spiːk jə
　'maɪnd/
take (your) mind off
　(something) (v) /teɪk jə
　maɪnd ɒf 'sʌmθɪŋ/

Expressions with *brain*

brainchild (n) /'breɪntʃaɪld/
brainstorm (v) /'breɪnstɔːm/
brainwave (n) /'breɪnweɪv/
have something on the brain
　(v) /hæv 'sʌmθɪŋ ɒn ðə
　breɪn/
pick someone's brain (v) /pɪk
　'sʌmwns breɪn/
super brain (n) /'suːpə breɪn/

Adjectives

detailed /'diːteɪld/
embarrassing /ɪm'bærəsɪŋ/
extraordinary /ɪk'strɔːdənərɪ/
remarkable /rɪ'mɑːkəbəl/
speechless /'spiːtʃləs/

unique /juː'niːk/
upset /ʌp'set/
upside /'ʌpsaɪd/

Nouns

architecture /'ɑːkɪtektʃə/
audience /'ɔːdiənts/
blockage /'blɒkɪdʒ/
factory /'fæktəri/
forehead /'fɔːhed/
hole /həʊl/
landmark /'lændmɑːk/
lawyer /'lɔɪə/
loaf /ləʊf/
prime number /'praɪm
　nʌmbə/
scratch /skrætʃ/
show /ʃəʊ/
slave /sleɪv/
square root /skweə 'ruːt/
suspicion /sə'spɪʃən/
viewer /vjuːə/

Verbs

appear /ə'pɪə/
beg /beɡ/
cause /kɔːz/
design /dɪ'zaɪn/
feature /'fiːtʃə/
groan /ɡrəʊn/
notice /'nəʊtɪs/
operate /'ɒpəreɪt/
perform /pə'fɔːm/
poke /pəʊk/
press /pres/
punish /'pʌnɪʃ/
react /ri'ækt/
realise /'rɪəlaɪz/
retire /rɪ'taɪə/
squat /skwɒt/
stack /stæk/
wrestle /'resl/
yell /jel/

Adverbs

immediately /ɪ'miːdiətli/
perfectly /'pɜːfɪktli/
properly /'prɒpəli/
seriously /'sɪəriəsli/

Unit 2

Health and medicine

anaesthetic (n) /ænəs'θetɪk/
cancer (n) /'kæntsə/
checkup (n) /'tʃekʌp/
cure (v, n) /kjʊə/
diagnosis (n) /,daɪəɡ'nəʊsɪs/

healer (n) /'hiːlə/
inject (v) /ɪn'dʒekt/
medication (n) /,medɪ'keɪʃən/
operate on (someone) (v)
　/'ɒpəreɪt ɒn sʌmwn/
operating theatre (n)
　/'ɒpəreɪtɪŋ 'θɪətə/
recover from (v) /rɪ'kʌvə
　frɒm/
remedy (n) /'remədi/
suffer from (v) /'sʌfə frɒm/
surgeon (n) /'sɜːdʒən/
symptom (n) /'sɪmptəm/
therapy (n) /'θerəpi/
treat (v) /triːt/
treatment (n) /'triːtmənt/
tumour (n) /'tjuːmə/

Flower remedies

holly (n) /'hɒli/
larch (n) /lɑːtʃ/
mustard (n) /'mʌstəd/
olive (n) /'ɒlɪv/
pine (n) /paɪn/
willow (n) /'wɪləʊ/

Feelings

absent-minded (adj) /,æbsənt
　'maɪndɪd/
homesick (adj) /'həʊmsɪk/
inattentive (adj) /ɪnə'tentɪv/
nostalgic (adj) /nɒs'tældʒɪk/
over-anxious (adj)
　/əʊvr'æŋkʃəs/
panicky (adj) /'pænɪki/

Adjectives

ancient /'eɪntʃənt/
anti-ageing /,ænti'eɪdʒɪŋ/
anxious /'æŋkʃəs/
astonished /ə'stɒnɪʃt/
chemical /'kemɪkəl/
effective /ɪ'fektɪv/
herbal /'hɜːbəl/
indigenous /ɪn'dɪdʒɪnəs/
miraculous /mɪ'rækjələs/
positive /'pɒzətɪv/
powerful /'paʊəfəl/
worthless /'wɜːθləs/

Nouns

arrow /'ærəʊ/
belief /bi'liːf/
imagery /'ɪmɪdʒəri/
ingredient /ɪn'griːdiənt/
instructor /ɪn'strʌktə/
jungle /dʒʌŋgl/
malaria /mə'leəriə/
mix /mɪks/

placebo /plə'siːbəʊ/
poison /'pɔɪzən/
quinine /'kwɪniːn/
tribe /traɪb/
value /'væljuː/
venom /'venəm/

Verbs

co-exist /kəʊɪɡ'zɪst/
derive /dɪ'raɪv/
develop /dɪ'veləp/
diminish /dɪ'mɪnɪʃ/
discover /dɪ'skʌvə/
dismiss /dɪ'smɪs/
melt /melt/
pass down /pɑːs daʊn/
produce /prə'djuːs/

Adverbs

botanically /bə'tænɪkəli/
frankly /'fræŋkli/
fully /'fʊli/
harmoniously /hɑː'məʊniəsli/
increasingly /ɪn'kriːsɪŋli/
potentially /pəʊ'tentʃəli/
systematically
　/,sɪstə'mætɪkəli/
traditionally /trə'dɪʃənəli/
typically /'tɪpɪkəli/

Everyday English

easier said than done /'iːzɪə
　sed ðæn dʌn/
how come ...? /haʊ 'kʌm/
how on earth? /haʊ ɒn 'ɜːθ/
off your trolley /ɒf jə 'trɒli/
you're well on your way /jɔː
　'wel ɒn jə weɪ/

Unit 3

Sports

amateur (n) /'æmətə/
board (n) /bɔːd/
boxer (n) /'bɒksə/
boxing (n) /'bɒksɪŋ/
boxing match (n) /'bɒksɪŋ
　mætʃ/
competitive (adj)
　/kəm'petɪtɪv/
court (n) /kɔːt/
defender (n) /dɪ'fendə/
draw (n) /drɔː/
glove (n) /ɡlʌv/
goal (n) /ɡəʊl/
goggles (n) /'ɡɒɡlz/
helmet (n) /'helmət/
hockey stick (n) /hɒki stɪk/

ice hockey (n) /aɪs 'hɒki/
lose (v) /luːz/
match (n) /mætʃ/
net (n) /net/
pitch (n) /pɪtʃ/
pool (n) /puːl/
puck (n) /pʌk/
racing car (n) /reɪsɪŋ kɑː/
racket (n) /'rækɪt/
ring (n) /rɪŋ/
rink (n) /rɪŋk/
score (v) /skɔː/
send off (v) /send ɒf/
skate (n) /skeɪt/
spectator (n) /spek'teɪtə/
swimming cap (n) /'swɪmɪŋ kæp/
team-mate (n) /tiːmmeɪt/
win (v) /wɪn/

Adjectives

academic /ˌækə'demɪk/
aggressive /ə'gresɪv/
balanced /'bæləntst/
biological /ˌbaɪə'lɒdʒɪkəl/
clear /klɪə/
effective /ɪ'fektɪv/
facial /'feɪʃəl/
long-term /ˌlɒŋ'tɜːm/
mechanical /mɪ'kænɪkəl/
newborn /njuː'bɔːn/
non-verbal /nɒn'vɜːbəl/
profound /prə'faʊnd/
rational /'ræʃənəl/
recent /'riːsənt/
scientific /ˌsaɪən'tɪfɪk/
subtle /'sʌtl/
superior /suː'pɪəriə/

Nouns

aggression /ə'greʃən/
brain damage /breɪn 'dæmɪdʒ/
communication skill
    /kəˌmjuːnɪ'keɪʃən skɪl/
concept /'kɒnsept/
concern /kən'sɜːn/
construction industry
    /kən'strʌkʃən 'ɪndəstri/
device /dɪ'vaɪs/
empathy /'empəθi/
engineering /ˌendʒi'nɪərɪŋ/
gender /'dʒendə/
knowledge /'nɒlɪdʒ/
lab /læb/
outlet /'aʊtlet/
skill /skɪl/
stereotype /'sterɪəʊtaɪp/
strength /strenkθ/
study /'stʌdi/
upbringing /'ʌpˌbrɪŋɪŋ/
weakness /'wiːknəs/
wisdom /'wɪzdəm/

Verbs

acquire /ə'kwaɪə/

comfort /'kʌmpfət/
conduct /kən'dʌkt/
differ /'dɪfə/
emphasize /'empfəsaɪz/
engage (in) /ɪn'geɪdʒ/
flip /flɪp/
include /ɪn'kluːd/
judge /dʒʌdʒ/
recognise /'rekəgnaɪz/
reinforce /ˌriːɪn'fɔːs/
relate (to) /rɪ'leɪt/
require /rɪ'kwaɪə/
respond /rɪ'spɒnd/
suggest /sə'dʒest/
tend (to) /tend/
value /'væljuː/

Adverbs

clearly /'klɪəli/
fundamentally
    /ˌfʌndə'mentəli/
generally /'dʒenərəli/
highly /'haɪli/
personally /'pɜːsənəli/

Unit 4

Expressions with *time*

give (someone) a hard time
    /gɪv sʌmwʌn ə hɑːd taɪm/
have time to /hæv taɪm/
in time /ɪn taɪm/
on time /ɒn taɪm/
run out of time /rʌn aʊt əv
    taɪm/
spend time /spend taɪm/
take time off /teɪk taɪm ɒf/
take your time /teɪk jə taɪm/
waste time /weɪst taɪm/

Reporting verbs

advise (someone) to /əd'vaɪz/
claim (that) /kleɪm/
convince (someone) not to
    /kən'vɪnts/
deny (that) /dɪnaɪ/
emphasise (that) /'empfəsaɪz/
encourage /ɪn'kʌrɪdʒ/
persuade (someone) not to
    /pə'sweɪd/
promise (not) to /'prɒmɪs/
recommend /ˌrekə'mend/
refuse to /rɪfjuːz/
state (that) /steɪt/
suggest (that) /sə'dʒest/
warn (someone) that /wɔːn/

Adjectives

charismatic /ˌkærɪz'mætɪk/
concerned /kən'sɜːnd/
convenient /kən'viːniənt/
cult /kʌlt/
disappointed /ˌdɪsə'pɔɪntɪd/
enthusiastic /ɪnˌθjuːzi'æstɪk/

familiar /fə'mɪliə/
fed up /fed ʌp/
key /kiː/
pleasant /'plezənt/
pushy /'pʊʃi/
stressed out /strest aʊt/

Nouns

arrangement /ə'reɪndʒmənt/
claim /kleɪm/
denial /dɪ'naɪəl/
encouragement
    /ɪn'kʌrɪdʒmənt/
genre /'ʒɑːnrə/
lord /lɔːd/
rebirth /ˌriː'bɜːθ/
recommendation
    /ˌrekəmen'deɪʃən/
refusal /rɪ'fjuːzəl/
sidekick /'saɪdkɪk/
time traveller /taɪm 'trævələ/
universe /'juːnɪvɜːs/
warning /'wɔːnɪŋ/
warrior /'wɒriə/
weapon /'wepən/

Verbs

avoid /ə'vɔɪd/
broadcast /'brɔːdkɑːst/
depend on /dɪ'pend ɒn/
drop out /drɒp aʊt/
greet /griːt/
meditate /'medɪteɪt/
overtake /ˌəʊvə'teɪk/
send away /send ə'weɪ/
swear /sweə/
tear apart /teə ə'pɑːt/
wound /wuːnd/

Adverbs

completely /kəm'pliːtli/
healthily /helθili/
honestly /'ɒnɪstli/
probably /'prɒbəbli/

Unit 5

Personality adjectives

arrogant /'ærəgənt/
bubbly /'bʌbli/
careless /'keələs/
charming /'tʃɑːmɪŋ/
cheeky /'tʃiːki/
hypocritical /ˌhɪpəʊ'krɪtɪkəl/
intellectual /ˌɪntəl'ektjuəl/
pretentious /prɪ'tentʃəs/
pushy /'pʊʃi/
scatty /'skæti/
sensible /sentsɪbl/
shallow /'ʃæləʊ/
smug /smʌg/
sympathetic /ˌsɪmpə'θetɪk/
violent /'vaɪələnt/
witty /'wɪti/

Adjectives

awkward /'ɔːkwəd/
choosy /'tʃuːzi/
disagreeable /ˌdɪsə'griːəbl/
enchanting /ɪn'tʃɑːntɪŋ/
gorgeous /'gɔːdʒəs/
insupportable /ˌɪnsə'pɔːtəbl/
playful /'pleɪfəl/
plump /plʌmp/
scruffy /'skrʌfi/
ridiculous /rɪ'dɪkjələs/
tolerable /'tɒlərəbl/

Nouns

anxiety /æŋ'zaɪəti/
disposition /ˌdɪspə'zɪʃən/
gossip /'gɒsɪp/
impression /ɪm'preʃən/
manner /'mænə/
nightmare /'naɪtmeə/
phenomenon /fɪ'nɒmɪnən/
presentation /ˌprezən'teɪʃən/
stain /steɪn/

Verbs

acquaint yourself with
    /ə'kweɪnt jəself wɪð/
blush /blʌʃ/
consider /kən'sɪdə/
cover up /kʌvə ʌp/
decline to /dɪ'klaɪn/
delight in /dɪ'laɪt/
dislike /dɪ'slaɪk/
exaggerate /ɪg'zædʒəreɪt/
ignore /ɪg'nɔː/
impress /'ɪmpres/
in no mood to (do) /ɪn'nəʊ
    muːd/
manage /'mænɪdʒ/
obliged to (do) /ə'blaɪdʒd/
offend /ə'fend/
overcome /ˌəʊvə'kʌm/
show (someone) round /ʃəʊ
    raʊnd/
tell (someone) off /tel ɒf/
tempt /tempt/

Adverbs

certainly /'sɜːtənli/
coldly /'kəʊldli/
definitely /'defɪnətli/

Unit 6

Adverbial phrases

by accident /baɪ 'æksɪdənt/
in a hurry /ɪn ə 'hʌri/
in a panic /ɪn ə 'pænɪk/
in a row /ɪn ə raʊ/
in private /ɪn 'praɪvɪt/
in public /ɪn 'pʌblɪk/
in secret /ɪn 'siːkrət/
on purpose /ɒn 'pɜːpəs/

Adjectives

addictive /əˈdɪktɪv/
anonymous /əˈnɒnɪməs/
biased /ˈbaɪəst/
compulsive /kəmˈpʌlsɪv/
digital /ˈdɪdʒɪtəl/
enjoyable /ɪnˈdʒɔɪəbl/
instantaneous /ˌɪntstənˈteɪnɪəs/
mass /mæs/
moral /ˈmɒrəl/
narrow-minded /ˌnærəʊˈmaɪndɪd/
potential /pəˈtentʃəl/
provocative /prəˈvɒkətɪv/
reluctant /rɪˈlʌktənt/
short-lived /ʃɔːtˈlɪvd/
useless /ˈjuːsləs/

Nouns

commerce /ˈkɒmɜːs/
craze /kreɪz/
creativity /ˌkriːeɪˈtɪvəti/
cube /kjuːb/
disc /dɪsk/
flash mob /flæʃ mɒb/
frisbee /ˈfrɪzbi/
housewife /ˈhaʊswaɪf/
hula hoop /ˈhuːlə huːp/
marketing /ˈmɑːkɪtɪŋ/
mini-riot /ˈmɪni raɪət/
multimillionaire /ˌmʌltimɪljəˈneə/
period /ˈpɪəriəd/
production /prəˈdʌkʃən/
puzzle /ˈpʌzl/
rug /rʌg/
shopkeeper /ˈʃɒpˌkiːpə/
spread /spred/
sociologist /ˌsəʊʃiˈɒlədʒɪst/
sunflower /ˈsʌnflaʊə/
tamagotchi /ˌtæməˈgɒtʃi/
teddy bear /ˈtedi beə/
tendency /ˈtendəntsi/
tube /tjuːb/

Verbs

ban /bæn/
be grateful that /biː greɪtfl ðæt/
be reluctant to /biː rɪˈlʌktənt/
beware /bɪˈweə/ (imperative form only)
catch on /kætʃ ɒn/
dare /deə/
extend /ɪkˈstend/
feed /fiːd/
fiddle /ˈfɪdl/
grow up /grəʊ ʌp/
mug /mʌg/
produce /ˈprɒdjuːs/
queue up /kjuː ʌp/
solve /sɒlv/
suspend /səˈspend/

sweep through /swiːp θruː/
take part in /teɪk pɑːt ɪn/
take up (space) /taɪk ʌp/
throw (something) away /θrəʊ əˈweɪ/
throw (something) out /θrəʊ aʊt/
turn up /tɜːn ʌp/
twirl /twɜːl/

Adverbs

angrily /ˈæŋgrɪli/
easily /ˈiːzli/
excitedly /ɪkˈsaɪtɪdli/
intentionally /ɪnˈtentʃənəli/
loudly /ˈlaʊdli/
patiently /ˈpeɪʃəntli/
suddenly /ˈsʌdənli/
surprisingly /səˈpraɪzɪŋli/

Everyday English

Besides, ... /bɪˈsaɪdz/
For a start, ... /fɔː ə ˈstɑːt/
out of order /aʊt ɒv ˈɔːdə/
real /rɪəl/

Unit 7

Making an effort

struggle with (something) (v) /ˈstrʌgəl wɪð/
do (something) properly (v) /duː ˈprɒpəli/
do (something) wrong (v) /duː rɒŋ/
trial and error (n) /traɪəl nd ˈerə/
half-heartedly (adv) /ˌhɑːfˈhɑːtɪdli/
go to great lengths (v) /gəʊ tuː greɪt leŋkθs/
get a lot out of (something) (v) /get ə lɒt aʊt ɒv/
find (something) easy (v) /faɪnd ˈiːzi/

Adjectives

geographical /ˌdʒiːəʊˈgræfɪkəl/
shining /ˈʃaɪnɪŋ/
sparkling /ˈspɑːklɪŋ/
standard /ˈstændəd/
suspicious /səˈspɪʃəs/
unexpected /ˌʌnɪkˈspektɪd/
worldwide /wɜːldˈwaɪd/

Nouns

advert (ad) /ˈædvɜːt/ (/æd/)
barrier /ˈbæriə/
boundary /ˈbaʊndəri/
ceiling /ˈsiːlɪŋ/
deed /diːd/
detergent /dɪˈtɜːdʒənt/

expert /ˈekspɜːt/
goodies (plural) /ˈgʊdiːz/
headquarters /ˌhedˈkwɔːtəz/
kindness /ˈkaɪndnəs/
Londoner /ˈlʌndənə/
noodle /ˈnuːdl/
passion for (something) /ˈpæʃən fɔː/
pinch /pɪntʃ/
rack /ræk/
shrine /ʃraɪn/
stranger /ˈstreɪndʒə/
streamer /ˈstriːmə/
tradition /trəˈdɪʃən/
waltz /wɒlts/

Verbs

acknowledge /əkˈnɒlɪdʒ/
admit /ədˈmɪt/
approve /əˈpruːv/
blindfold /ˈblaɪndfəʊld/
carry out /kæri ˈaʊt/
chat /tʃæt/
congratulate /kənˈgrætʃʊleɪt/
contain /kənˈteɪn/
correspond /ˌkɒrɪˈspɒnd/
experiment /ɪkˈsperɪmənt/
get on /get ɒn/
speak out /spiːk aʊt/
step /step/
walk away /wɑːk əˈweɪ/
walk up (to someone) /wɔːk ʌp/
wash up /wɒʃ ʌp/

Adverbs

properly /ˈprɒpəli/
simply /ˈsɪmpli/

Unit 8

War and peace

army (n) /ˈɑːmi/
assassinate (v) /əˈsæsɪneɪt/
blast (v) /blɑːst/
bomb (n) /bɒm/
dynamite (n) /ˈdaɪnəmaɪt/
explode (v) /ɪkˈspləʊd/
explosion (n) /ɪkˈspləʊʒən/
explosive (n) /ɪkˈspləʊsɪv/
landmine (n) /ˈlændmaɪn/
military (adj) /ˈmɪlɪtri/
non-violent (adj) /nɒnˈvaɪələnt/
peaceful (adj) /ˈpiːsfəl/
peace (n) /piːs/
prisoner (n) /ˈprɪzənə/
weapon (n) /ˈwepən/

Conflicts and solutions

fall out (v) /fɔːl ˈaʊt/

find a solution (v) /faɪnd ə səˈluːʃən/
get stuck (v) /get ˈstʌk/
make up (v) /meɪk ʌp/
reach a compromise (v) /riːtʃ ə ˈkɒmprəmaɪz/
resolve conflicts (v) /rɪˈzɒlv ˈkɒnflɪkts/
sort things out (v) /ˈsɔːt θɪŋz aʊt/
stay neutral (v) /steɪ ˈnjuːtrəl/
take sides (v) /ˈteɪk saɪdz/

Adjectives

downhearted /ˌdaʊnˈhɑːtɪd/
effective /ɪˈfektɪv/
immediate /ɪˈmiːdiət/
overwhelmed /ˌəʊvəˈwelmd/
political /pəˈlɪtɪkəl/

Nouns

ambassador /æmˈbæsədə/
conference /ˈkɒnfərənts/
deadlock /ˈdedlɒk/
democracy /dɪˈmɒkrəsi/
dictatorship /dɪkˈteɪtəʃip/
government /ˈgʌvənment/
handkerchief /ˈhæŋkətʃiːf/
hatred /ˈheɪtrɪd/
house arrest /haʊs əˈrest/
human rights /ˈhjuːmən raɪts/
ideal /aɪˈdɪəl/
insanity /ɪnˈsænəti/
invention /ɪnˈventʃn/
prejudice /ˈpredʒədɪs/
prime minister /praɪm ˈmɪnɪstə/
natural resources /ˈnætʃərəl rɪˈzɔːsɪz/
nitro-glycerine /naɪtrəʊ ˈglɪsəriːn/
Nobel peace prize /nəʊˈbel piːs praɪz/
obituary /əʊˈbɪtʃʊəri/
opposition leader /ˌɒpəˈzɪʃən liːdə/
path /pɑːθ/
protestor /prəʊˈtestə/
rule /ruːl/

Verbs

abolish /əˈbɒlɪʃ/
accuse /əˈkjuːz/
award /əˈwɔːd/
confront /kənˈfrʌnt/
free /friː/
invent /ɪnˈvent/
manage /ˈmænɪdʒ/
manufacture /ˌmænjəˈfæktʃə/
nominate /ˈnɒmɪneɪt/
print /prɪnt/
produce /prədjuːs/
promote /prəˈməʊt/
protest /ˈprəʊtest/

receive /rɪ'siːv/
reward /rɪ'wɔːd/
slip away /slɪp ə'weɪ/
sort out /sɔːt aʊt/
take away /taɪk ə'weɪ/

Adverbs

accidentally /ˌæksɪ'dentəli/
courageously /kə'reɪdʒəsli/

Unit 9

Ways of getting involved

do some volunteer work /duː sʌm ˌvɒlən'tɪə wɜːk/
get sponsored /get 'spɒntsəd/
go on a demonstration /gəʊ ɒn ə ˌdemən'streɪʃən/
hand out leaflets /hænd aʊt 'liːfləts/
make a donation /meɪk ə dəʊ'neɪʃən/
sign a petition /saɪn ə pə'tɪʃən/

Adjectives

corrupt /kə'rʌpt/
delicate /'delɪkət/
dreary /'drɪəri/
eager /'iːgə/
immature /ˌɪmə'tjʊə/
individual /ˌɪndɪ'vɪdʒʊəl/
institutional /ˌɪntstɪ'tjuːʃənəl/
obvious /'ɒbvɪəs/
specific /spə'sɪfɪk/
traceable /'treɪsəbl/
uphill /ʌp'hɪl/
voluntary /'vɒləntri/

Nouns

altitude /'æltɪtjuːd/
applause /ə'plɔːz/
arrogance /'ærəgənts/
ascent /ə'sent/
banner /'bænə/
base camp /'beɪs kæmp/
blanket /'blæŋkɪt/
choir /kwaɪə/
clamour /'klæmə/
conch /kɒntʃ/
current issue /'kʌrənt ɪʃuː/
day off /'deɪ ɒf/
demonstration /ˌdemən'streɪʃən/
election /ɪ'lekʃən/
finish line /'fɪnɪʃ laɪn/
head boy /hed 'bɔɪ/
leaflet /'liːflət/
lottery /'lɒtəri/
marathon /'mærəθən/
obedience /əʊ'biːdɪənts/
publicity /pʌb'lɪsəti/

racism /'reɪsɪzəm/
rest day /'rest deɪ/
route /ruːt/
runner /'rʌnə/
shell /ʃel/
stillness /'stɪlnəs/
suspension bridge /sə'spentʃən brɪdʒ/
tax /tæks/
trunk /trʌŋk/
voter /'vəʊtə/

Verbs

applaud /ə'plɔːd/
change /tʃeɪndʒ/
contribute /kən'trɪbjuːt/
hesitate /'hezɪteɪt/
hike /haɪk/
organise /'ɔːgənaɪz/
raise /reɪz/
stir /stɜː/
suppose /sə'pəʊz/
upload /ʌp'ləʊd/
vote /vəʊt/

Adverbs

absently /'æbsəntli/
grudgingly /'grʌdʒɪŋli/
obscurely /əb'skjʊəli/
powerfully /'paʊəfəli/
sensibly /'sentsɪbli/
timidly /'tɪmɪdli/

Unit 10

Global issues

atmosphere (n) /'ætməsfɪə/
bring about (v) /brɪŋ ə'baʊt/
die out (v) /'daɪ aʊt/
foul up (v) /'faʊl ʌp/
get rid of (v) /get' 'rɪd əf/
go up by (v) /gəʊ 'ʌp baɪ/
natural resources (n) /'nætʃərəl rɪ'zɔːsɪz/
solar panel (n) /'səʊlə 'pænəl/
starvation (n) /stɑː'veɪʃən/
temperature (n) /'temprətʃə/
use up (v) /juːs ʌp/
waste (n) /weɪst/

Conserving energy

conventional (adj) /kən'ventʃənəl/
cut down on (v) /kʌt 'daʊn ɒn/
electrical appliance (n) /ɪˌlektrɪkəl ə'plaɪnts/
light bulb (n) /'laɪt ˌbʌlb/
long-life (adj) /'lɒŋlaɪf/
microwave oven (n) /ˌmaɪkrəʊweɪv 'ʌvən/
recycle (v) /ˌriː'saɪkəl/
swap (v) /swɒp/
switch off (v) /swɪtʃ 'ɒf/
unplug (v) /ʌn'plʌg/

Adjectives

ahead /ə'hed/
conventional /kən'ventʃənəl/
deadly /'dedli/
disgusting /dɪs'gʌstɪŋ/
ecological /ˌiːkə'lɒdʒɪkəl/
flexible /'fleksɪbl/
gloomy /'gluːmi/
undersea /ˌʌndə'siː/

Nouns

category /'kætəgəri/
cod /kɒd/
data /'deɪtə/
diesel /'diːzəl/
ecological footprint /ˌiːkə'lɒdʒɪkəl 'fʊtprɪnt/
fresh water supply (n) /freʃ 'wɔːtə 'sʌpli/
fuel /'fjuːəl/
headline /'hedlaɪn/
hectare /'hekteə/
liquid /'lɪkwɪd/
mankind /mæn'kaɪnd/
nuclear waste (n) /'njuːklɪə weɪst/
outer space /'aʊtə speɪs/
packet /'pækɪt/
pet food /pet fuːd/
petrol /'petrəl/
rain water /'reɪnˌwɔːtə/
replacement /rɪ'pleɪsmənt/
source (n) /sɔːs/
species (n) /'spiːʃiːz/

Verbs

abuse /ə'bjuːz/
blame /bleɪm/
colonise /'kɒlənaɪz/
consume /kən'sjuːm/
dispose of /dɪ'spəʊz ɒv/
exploit /'eksplɔɪt/
get rid of /'get rɪd ɒv/
measure /'meʒə/
pollute /pə'luːt/
predict /prɪ'dɪkt/
reduce /rɪ'djuːs/
take (something) seriously /taɪk 'sɪəriəsli/
tick along /tɪk ə'lɒŋ/
vanish /'vænɪʃ/

Adverbs

hopefully /'həʊpfəli/
particularly /pə'tɪkjələi/
unsurprisingly /ʌnsə'praɪzɪŋi/

Everyday English

Come off it! /kʌm ɒf ɪt/
Point taken. /pɔɪnt 'teɪkən/
Since when? /sɪnts 'hwen/
So what? /səʊ hwɒt/
stuff like that /'stʌf laɪk ðæt/

Unit 11

Fame

be famous for (v) /'feɪməs fɔː/
celebrity (n) /se'ləbrəti/
enjoy a lot of success (v) /ɪn'dʒɔɪ ə lɒt ɒv sək'ses/
household name (n) /'haʊshəʊld neɪm/
make it big (v) /meɪk ɪt bɪg/
media star (n) /'miːdɪə stɑː/
singing sensation (n) /'sɪŋɪŋ sen'seɪʃən/

Expressing opinions

As far as I'm concerned /æz fɑː æz aɪm kən'sɜːnd/
I couldn't care less /aɪ 'kʊdənt keə les/
I'd have thought (that) /aɪd əv θɔːt ðæt/
If you ask me /ɪf juː 'ɑːsk miː/
In my opinion /ɪn maɪ ə'pɪnjən/
The way I see it /ðə weɪ 'aɪ siː ɪt/
To my mind /tuː 'maɪ maɪnd/

Adjectives

glossy /'glɒsi/
harmful /'hɑːmfəl/
homeless /'həʊmləs/
humanitarian /hjuːˌmænɪ'teəriən/
professional /prə'feʃənl/
prosperous /'prɒspərəs/
starving /'stɑːvɪŋ/
strict /strɪkt/
superficial /ˌsuːpə'fɪʃəl/

Nouns

aid /eɪd/
agency /'eɪdʒəntsi/
ambassador /æm'bæsədə/
awareness /ə'weənəs/
background music /'bækgraʊnd 'mjuːzɪk/
cancellation /ˌkæntsəl'eɪʃən/
chat show /tʃæt ʃəʊ/
commitment /kə'mɪtmənt/
debt /det/
debut /'deɪbjuː/
disappointment /ˌdɪsə'pɔɪntmənt/
famine /'fæmɪn/
follow-up /'fɒləʊʌp/
gig /gɪg/
instigator /'ɪntstɪgeɪtə/
leader /'liːdə/
mission /'mɪʃən/
organiser /'ɔːgənaɪzə/
poverty /'pɒvəti/
refugee /ˌrefjʊ'dʒiː/

relief /rɪ'liːf/
safety /'seɪfti/
spokeswoman /'spəʊks,wʊmən/
status /'steɪtəs/
victim /'vɪktɪm/

Verbs

accompany /ə'kʌmpəni/
coincide /,kəʊɪn'saɪd/
combine /'kɒmbaɪn/
distract /dɪ'strækt/
donate /dəʊ'neɪt/
ensure /ɪn'ʃɔː/
estimate /'estɪmeɪt/
focus /'fəʊkəs/
identify /aɪ'dentɪfaɪ/
perceive /pə'siːv/
recruit /rɪ'kruːt/
represent /,reprɪ'zent/
seek /siːk/
spread (the word) /spred/

Adverbs

continually /kən'tɪnjuəli/
globally /'gləʊbəli/
internationally /,ɪntə'næʃnəli/
massively /'mæsɪvli/
obviously /'ɒbviəsli/

Unit 12

Phrasal verbs

back up /'bæk ʌp/
bring round /brɪŋ 'raʊnd/
come across /kʌm ə'krɒs/
give back /gɪv 'bæk/
go up /gəʊ' ʌp/
live on /'lɪv ɒn/
make (something) up /meɪk 'ʌp/
make up for (something) /meɪk 'ʌp fə/
send off /send' ɒf/
take back /teɪk' bæk/
take off /'teɪk ɒf/

Adjectives

basic /'beɪsɪk/
brief /briːf/
educational /,edʒuː'keɪʃənəl/
entire /ɪn'taɪə/
minimum /'mɪnɪməm/
trendy /'trendi/
unconscious /ʌn'kɒntʃəs/

Nouns

bank account /bæŋk ə'kaʊnt/
canteen /kæn'tiːn/
community /kə'mjuːnəti/
consumer /kən'sjuːmə/
diary /'daɪəri/

---

establishment /ɪ'stæblɪʃmənt/
fair trade /feə 'treɪd/
guarantee /,gærən'tiː/
label /'leɪbəl/
outcome /'aʊtkʌm/
principle /'prɪntsəpl/
product /'prɒdʌkt/
proportion /prə'pɔːʃən/
regulation /,regjə'leɪʃən/
robbery /'rɒbəri/
sanitation /,sænɪ'teɪʃən/
wage /weɪdʒ/
wealth /welθ/

Verbs

aim /eɪm/
be prepared to (do something) /bi: prɪ'peəd tuː/
benefit /'benɪfɪt/
claim /kleɪm/
combat /'kɒmbæt/
control /kən'trəʊl/
deserve /dɪ'zɜːv/
ensure /ɪn'ʃɔː/
import /ɪm'pɔːt/
invest /ɪn'vest/
label /'leɪbəl/
prove /pruːv/
recognise /'rekəgnaɪz/

Adverbs

financially /faɪ'næntʃəli/
regularly /'regjələli/
suspiciously /sə'spɪʃəsli/
tragically /'trædʒɪkli/

Unit 13

Communication

accent (n) /'æksnt/
clarify (v) /'klærɪfaɪ/
communicate (v) /kə'mjuːnɪkeɪt/
consonant (n) /'kɒntsənənt/
internet (n) /'ɪntənet/
message (n) /'mesɪdʒ/
misunderstand (v) /,mɪsʌndə'stænd/
misunderstanding (n) /mɪsʌndə'stændɪŋ/
mobile phone (n) /məʊbaɪl 'fəʊn/
pronunciation (n) /prə,nʌntsi'eɪʃən/
refer to (v) /rɪ'fɜː/
vowel (n) /vaʊəl/
whistle (v) /'wɪsl/

Understanding language

get some of ... /get sʌm ɒv/
get the gist of (something) /get ðə 'dʒɪst ɒv/

---

incomprehensible /ɪn,kɒmprɪ'hentsəbl/
lose (someone) completely /luːz kəm'pliːtli/
(not) catch (something) /kætʃ/
(not) make out anything at all /meɪk aʊt 'eniθɪŋ æt ɔːl/
manage to pick a few words out /'mænɪdʒ tuː pɪk ə fjuː wɜːdz aʊt/
(not) understand a word of ... . /,ʌndə'stænd ə wɜːd əv/

Adjectives

appropriate /ə'prəʊpriət/
bloated /'bləʊtɪd/
compulsory /kəm'pʌlsəri/
cultural /'kʌltʃərəl/
fearful /'fɪəfəl/
giant /'dʒaɪənt/
historical /hɪ'stɒrɪkəl/
linguistic /lɪŋ'gwɪstɪk/
mountainous /'maʊntɪnəs/
offshore /,ɒf'ʃɔː/
slight /slaɪt/
slimy /'slaɪmi/
vile /vaɪl/

Nouns

beast /biːst/
betrayal /bɪ'treɪəl/
birdsong /'bɜːd'sɒŋ/
breed /briːd/
changing room /'tʃeɪndʒɪŋ ruːm/
depression /dɪ'preʃən/
distance /'dɪstənts/
edge /edʒ/
educator /'edʒʊkeɪtə/
exhibition /,eksɪ'bɪʃən/
extinction /ɪk'stɪŋkʃən/
foam /fəʊm/
fortnight /'fɔːtnaɪt/
heritage /'herɪtɪdʒ/
keks (shorts) /keks/
origin /'ɒrɪdʒɪn/
toad /təʊd/
undertow /'ʌndətəʊ/

Verbs

declare /dɪ'kleə/
drag away /dræg ə'weɪ/
dread /dred/
drown /draʊn/
evoke /ɪ'vəʊk/
howl /haʊl/
lend /lend/
lurk /lɜːk/
originate /ə'rɪdʒəneɪt/
peer /pɪə/
preserve /prɪ'zɜːv/
ravage /'rævɪdʒ/
recall /rɪ'kɔːl/
retreat /rɪ'triːt/
snare /sneə/

---

trek /trek/
venture /'ventʃə/

Adverbs

exactly /ɪg'zæktli/
fortunately /'fɔːtʃənətli/
respectfully /rɪ'spektfəl/
unfortunately /ʌn'fɔːtʃənətli/

Unit 14

Geographical features

bay /beɪ/
canyon /'kænjən/
cliff /klɪf/
coral reef /'kɒrəl riːf/
desert /'dezət/
glacier /'glæsiə/
lake /leɪk/
mountain range /'maʊntɪn reɪndʒ/
plain /pleɪn/
waterfall /'wɔːtəfɔːl/

Travel verbs

get back to (the hotel) /get bæk tuː/
get in / out of (a car) /get ɪn/aʊt ɒv/
get on / off (a plane] /get ɒn/ɒf/
go away /gəʊ ə'weɪ/
go for (a drive) /gəʊ fɔː/
go on (a journey) /'gəʊ ɒn/
leave for /'liːv fɔː/
set off /'set ɒf/
take off /'teɪk ɒf/
drive off /'draɪv ɒf/
ride off /raɪd ɒf/

Adjectives

dim /dɪm/
gentle /'dʒentl/
greyish /'greɪɪʃ/
heavenly /'hevənli/
juicy /'dʒuːsi/
man-made /mænmaɪd/
marine /mə'riːn/
phosphorescent /,fɒsfər'esənt/
spectacular /spek'tækjələ/

Nouns

campground /'kæmpgraʊnd/
chaos /'keɪɒs/
concentration /,kɒntsən'treɪʃən/
ending /'endɪŋ/
glow /gləʊ/
magnetic field /mæg'netɪk fiːld/
medieval /,medi'iːvəl/
natural wonder /'nætʃərəl 'wʌndə/

particle /ˈpɑːtɪkl/
polyp /ˈpɒlɪp/
poster /ˈpəʊstə/
rim /rɪm/
roar /rɔː/
screech /skriːtʃ/
skeleton /ˈskelɪtən/
snorkelling /ˈsnɔːkəlɪŋ/
vacation /vəˈkeɪʃən/
whale shark /ˈhweɪl ʃɑːk/

Verbs

amaze /əˈmeɪz/
book /bʊk/
check in /tʃek ˈɪn/
interact /ˈɪntəækt/
overlook /ˌəʊvəˈlʊk/
rush out /rʌʃ aʊt/
sail down /seɪl daʊn/
shine /ʃaɪn/
stretch /stretʃ/

Everyday English

a bit of a nightmare /ə bɪt əf
ə ˈnaɪtmeə/
Get out of here! /get ˈaʊt əf
hɪə/
How does that grab you? /haʊ
dʌz ˈðæt græb juː/
Take it easy! /teɪk ɪt ˈiːzi/

Unit 15

Movie industry

box-office success (n) /ˈbɒks
ˌɒfɪs səkˈses/
character (n) /ˈkærəktə/
feature film (n) /ˈfiːtʃə fɪlm/
film goer (n) /fɪlm ˈgəʊə/
film-maker (n) /ˈfɪlm meɪkə/
hit (n) /hɪt/
plot (n) /plɒt/
profit (n) /ˈprɒfɪt/
romantic comedy (n)
/rəʊˈmæntɪk kɒmədi/
screen (n) /skriːn/

script (n) /skrɪpt/
sell out (n) /ˈsel aʊt/
set (n) /set/
shoot (v) (a scene) /ʃuːt/

Reacting to films

be on the edge of your seat
/biː ɒn ðə ˈedʒ ɒv jɔː
siːt/
bite your lip /baɪt ˈjɔː lɪp/
chuckle quietly /tʃʌkl
ˈkwaɪətli/
cry your eyes out /kraɪ jɔː
ˈaɪz aʊt/
fall about laughing /fɔːl
əˈbaʊt ˈlɑːfɪŋ/
jump out of your seat
/ˈdʒʌmp aʊt ɒv jɔː siːt/
scream /skriːm/
yawn /jɔːn/

Adjectives

alienated /ˈeɪliəneɪtɪd/
disastrous /dɪˈzɑːstrəs/
overdue /ˌəʊvəˈdjuː/
permanent /ˈpɜːmənənt/
therapeutic /ˌθerəˈpjuːtɪk/
trapped /træpt/
unfamiliar /ˌʌnfəˈmɪljə/
weekly /ˈwiːkli/

Nouns

approach /əˈprəʊtʃ/
approval /əˈpruːvəl/
bullet /ˈbʊlɪt/
catalyst /ˈkætəlɪst/
client /klaɪənt/
dilemma /dɪˈlemə/
flatmate /ˈflætmeɪt/
impact /ˈɪmpækt/
implication /ˌɪmplɪˈkeɪʃən/
jewellery /ˈdʒuːəlri/
method /ˈmeθəd/
millionaire /ˌmɪljəˈneə/
music chart /mjuːzɪk ˈtʃɑːt/
nickname /ˈnɪkneɪm/
piracy /ˈpaɪərəsi/

portray /pɔːˈtreɪ/
private school /ˈpraɪvɪt skuːl/
psychiatrist /saɪˈkaɪətrɪst/
psychotherapist
/ˌsaɪkəʊˈθerəpɪst/
session /ˈseʃən/
therapist /ˈθerəpɪst/
time bomb /taɪm bɒm/

Verbs

activate /ˈæktɪveɪt/
articulate /ɑːˈtɪkjəleɪt/
balance /ˈbælənts/
be desperate for /ˈdespərət/
chase /tʃeɪs/
clone /kləʊn/
counsel /ˈkaʊntsəl/
devote /ˈdɪvəʊt/
erupt /ɪˈrʌpt/
feature /ˈfiːtʃə/
lash out /læʃ aʊt/
nag /næg/
release /rɪˈliːs/
relive /ˌriːˈlɪv/
repress /rɪˈpres/
unlock /ʌnˈlɒk/

Unit 16

Listening to music

alphorn (n) /ˈælphɔːn/
bagpipes (n) /ˈbægpaɪps/
beat (n) /biːt/
berimbau (n) /bərɪmˈbaʊ/
bonang (n) /bəˈnæŋ/
classical music (n) /ˈklæsɪkəl
ˈmjuːzɪk/
didgeridoo (n) /ˌdɪdʒəriˈduː/
hum along (v) /hʌm əˈlɒŋ/
instrumental music (n)
/ˌɪntstrəˈmentəl
ˈmjuːzɪk/
live music (n) /laɪv ˈmjuːzɪk/
lyrics (n) /ˈlɪrɪks/
melody (n) /ˈmelədi/
muzak (n) /ˈmjuːzæk/

not be able to get (something)
out of your head (v) /get ɪt
aʊt ɒv jə ˈhed/
pulse (n) /pʌls/
recorded music (n) /rɪˈkɔːdid
ˈmjuːzɪk/
re-mix (n) /ˈriːmɪks/
rhyme (v) /raɪm/
rhythm (n) /ˈrɪðəm/
sing along (v) /sɪŋ əˈlɒŋ/
steel drum (n) /stiːl ˈdrʌm/
theme (n) /θiːm/
tune (n) /tjuːn/

Making comparisons stronger

even more /ˈiːvn mɔː/
far more /ˈfɑː mɔː/
just as /ˈdʒʌst æz/
a lot worse /ə lɒt ˈwɜːs/
much /mʌtʃ/
not nearly as /nɒt ˈnɪəli æz/
nothing like /ˈnʌθɪŋ laɪk/

Adjectives

humorous /ˈhjuːmərəs/

Nouns

agony /ˈægəni/
buyer /ˈbaɪə/
cabby /ˈkæbi/
courtyard /ˈkɔːtjɑːd/
entrance hall /ˈentrənts hɔːl/
limerick /ˈlɪmərɪk/
range /reɪndʒ/
skin /skɪn/
string /strɪŋ/

Verbs

clap /klæp/
complain /kəmˈpleɪn/
consult /kənˈsʌlt/
curve /kɜːv/
dry /draɪ/
hum /hʌm/

Phonetic symbols

Consonants					
/p/	pen	/m/	make	/j/	you
/b/	be	/n/	nice	/h/	he
/t/	two	/ŋ/	sing	/θ/	thing
/d/	do	/s/	see	/ð/	this
/k/	can	/z/	trousers	/ʃ/	she
/g/	good	/w/	we	/tʃ/	cheese
/f/	five	/l/	listen	/ʒ/	usually
/v/	very	/r/	right	/dʒ/	German

Vowels			
/æ/	man	/uː/	food
/ɑː/	father	/ʌ/	up
/e/	ten	/ɒ/	hot
/ɜː/	thirteen	/ɔː/	four
/ə/	mother		
/ɪ/	sit		
/iː/	see		
/ʊ/	book		

Diphthongs	
/eɪ/	great
/aɪ/	fine
/ɔɪ/	boy
/ɪə/	hear
/eə/	chair
/aʊ/	town
/əʊ/	go
/ʊə/	pure